GOOD NEWS
IS FOR SHARING

GOOD NEWS
IS FOR SHARING

8 sessions to encourage
and equip Christians
to share their personal faith
and communicate the Gospel

by Eddie Gibbs

VICTOR BOOKS
A DIVISION OF SCRIPTURE PRESS PUBLICATIONS INC.
USA CANADA ENGLAND

Recommended Dewey Decimal Classification: 301.402
Suggested Subject Heading: SMALL GROUPS

Library of Congress Catalog Card Number: 93-60864
ISBN: 1-56476-200-9

1   2   3   4   5   6   7   8   9   10   Printing/Year   98   97   96   95   94

VICTOR BOOKS
A division of SP Publications, Inc.
        Wheaton, Illinois 60187

CONTENTS

PURPOSE: To provide biblical insights, skill training, and group support so that we will have greater confidence and skill in sharing our faith.

INTRODUCTION 7

IS THIS YOUR FIRST SMALL GROUP? 9

SESSION 1—WHAT PRICE? 13
How Far God Was Prepared to Go on My Behalf

SESSION 2—EXPRESSING OUR GRATITUDE 23
A Message Too Important to Keep to Ourselves

SESSION 3—TREATING A TERMINAL CONDITION 33
Timely Interventions

SESSION 4—THIS IS MY STORY 43
Sharing My Experience of God's Love

SESSION 5—WHOM DO I KNOW? 53
Starting Close to Home

SESSION 6—TAKING TIME 65
Balancing Urgency with Patience

SESSION 7—CROSS TALK 75
Ways to Present the Gospel

SESSION 8—IT TAKES A COMMUNITY TO
COMMUNICATE 85
The Impact of Corporate Witness

DEAR SMALL GROUP LEADER 93
LEADER'S GUIDE 95

INTRODUCTION

Do I really want to get involved?

You're probably not alone in wondering what you are letting yourself into! It takes some courage to join a group which has undertaken to give serious consideration to faith sharing and communicating the Gospel. Joining a small group makes it difficult to assume "observer status"—you will be an active participant. It's not as safe as attending a seminar on the topic! But the problem with most seminars, and especially those relating to witnessing, is that when all is said and done, too much is said and too little is done.

The purpose of the 8 sessions of this course is for your group to learn together, encourage, and commiserate with one another as you learn at your own speed and in your own ways to share the Gospel. There is no "expert" present to intimidate by expecting everyone to display the same eagerness, aptitude, and effectiveness. Rather, you are here to stumble along together; to learn from each other's mistakes; to be enriched by the insights which the Lord gives as you study His Word and share your experiences; to support one another in first fumbling efforts and to rejoice at the unexpected breakthroughs.

The aim of this course is not just to gain information or to increase awareness. It is not designed to serve as a series of therapy sessions to deal with the guilt of neglect of, or failed attempts in, evangelism. It is designed to motivate each group member in evangelism and to improve evangelism skills. The anticipated outcome is more and better evangelization for the extension of Christ's kingdom and to the greater honor to His name.

An in-depth Leader's Guide is included at the back of the book with suggested time guidelines to help you structure your emphases. Each of the 8 sessions contains the following elements:

❑ **Getting Acquainted**—activities or selected readings to help you begin thinking and sharing from your life and experiences about the subject of the session. Use only those options that seem appropriate for your group.

❏ **Gaining Insight**—questions and in-depth Bible study help you gain principles from Scripture for life-related application.

❏ **Growing By Doing**—an opportunity to practice the Truth learned in the Gaining Insight section.

❏ **Going The Second Mile**—a personal enrichment section for you to do on your own.

❏ **Pocket Principles**—brief guidelines inserted in the Leader's Guide to help the Group Leader learn small group leadership skills as needed.

❏ **Session Objectives**—goals listed in the Leader's Guide that describe what should happen in the group by the end of the session.

Let us pray for one another that the message of the Lord may spread rapidly and be honored, just as it was with you (2 Thessalonians 3:1).

IS THIS YOUR FIRST SMALL GROUP?

'smol grüp: A limited number of individuals assembled together having some unifying relationship.

Kris'chen
'smol grüp: 4–12 persons who meet together on a regular basis, over a determined period of time, for the shared purpose of pursuing biblical truth. They seek to mature in Christ and become equipped to serve as His ministers in the world.

Picture Your First Small Group.

List some words that describe what you want your small group to look like.

What Kind Of Small Group Do You Have?

People form all kinds of groups based on gender, age, marital status, and so forth. There are advantages and disadvantages to each. Here are just a few:

❑ **Same Age Groups** will probably share similar needs and interests.

❑ **Intergenerational Groups** bring together people with different perspectives and life experiences.

❑ **Men's or Women's Groups** usually allow greater freedom in sharing and deal with more focused topics.

❑ **Singles or Married Groups** determine their relationship emphases based on the needs of a particular marital status.

❑ **Mixed Gender Groups (singles and/or couples)** stimulate interaction and broaden viewpoints while reflecting varied lifestyles.

However, the most important area of "alikeness" to consider when forming a group is an **agreed-on purpose.** Differences in purpose will sabotage your group and keep its members from bonding. If, for example, Mark wants to pray but not play while Jan's goal is to learn through playing, then Mark and Jan's group will probably not go anywhere. People need different groups at different times in their lives. Some groups will focus on sharing and accountability, some on work projects or service, and others on worship. *Your small group must be made up of persons who have similar goals.*

How Big Should Your Small Group Be?
The **fewest** people to include would be **4.** Accountability will be high, but absenteeism may become a problem.

The **most** to include would be **12.** But you will need to subdivide regularly into groups of 3 or 4 if you want people to feel cared for and to have time for sharing.

How Long Should You Meet?
8 Weeks gives you a start toward becoming a close community, but doesn't overburden busy schedules. Count on needing three or four weeks to develop a significant trust level. The smaller the group, the more quickly trust develops.

Weekly Meetings will establish bonding at a good pace and allow for accountability. The least you can meet and still be an effective group is once a month. If you choose the latter, work at individual contact among group members between meetings.

You will need **75 minutes** to accomplish a quality meeting. The larger the size, the more time it takes to become a healthy group. Serving refreshments will add 20–30 minutes, and singing and/or prayer time, another 20–30 minutes. Your time duration may be determined by the time of day you meet and by the amount of energy members bring to the group. Better to start small and ask for more time when it is needed because of growth.

What Will Your Group Do?
To be effective, each small group meeting should include:

1. **Sharing** — You need to share who you are and what is happening in your life. This serves as a basis for relationship building and becomes a springboard for searching out scriptural truth.

2. **Scripture** — There must always be biblical input from the Lord to teach, rebuke, correct, and train in right living. Such material serves to move your group in the direction of maturity in Christ and protects from pooled ignorance and distorted introspection.

3. **Truth in practice** — It is vital to provide opportunities for *doing* the Word of God. Experiencing this within the group insures greater likelihood that insights gained will be utilized in everyday living.

Other elements your group may wish to add to these three are: a time of **worship**, **specific prayer** for group members, **shared projects**, a time to **socialize** and enjoy **refreshments**, and **recreation**.

ONE

What Price?

How Far God Was Prepared to Go on My Behalf
Some people demonstrate tremendous heroism in fighting for a cause they believe in, or to save life. When a war is declared, some soldiers go reluctantly, under pressure, while others volunteer to serve and offer for the most dangerous assignments in the thick of the battle or behind enemy lines.

In the course of duty a police officer will confront an armed and dangerous criminal in order to secure the release of hostages. A firefighter will enter a burning building to save people trapped inside. Coastguard officers launch their vessels in the face of a howling gale and pounding seas in order to bring shipwrecked sailors and passengers safely to shore.

A passerby may dive into a fast-flowing river to rescue a drowning youth. A pedestrian leaps into the road to pull a child out of the path of oncoming traffic. But none of the human heroes can compare with God who chose to save us.

GETTING ACQUAINTED

Personal Involvement
What personal experiences do you have in fighting for a cause you believed in strongly?

13

❑ Working as a volunteer for a philanthropic organization, mission agency, or to lobby government.

❑ Yourself, or a family member, serving on active duty in the armed forces.

❑ Raising the alarm or personally engaging in a rescue attempt.

❑ An inspiring story you have heard about or which has received recent media attention concerning an act of heroism.

Our first session focuses on the greatest rescue operation of all time.

Thrills and Chills

If someone you loved were trapped in a burning building, you would probably rush in after that person without a second thought. Adrenaline would take over and you wouldn't have time to worry about feelings of inadequacy or fears for your own safety.

But when we attempt to be partners with God in rescuing others from a life without Christ, our emotions may be mixed. Picture yourself about to share your faith with someone. From the list below, check all the feelings you might have.

❑ Nervousness

❑ Exhilaration

❑ Fear of rejection

❑ Fear of failure

❑ Joy

❑ Embarrassment

❑ Other: _____

GAINING INSIGHT

Reconciled to God

John chapter three records the conversation which took place between Jesus and Nicodemus, the Pharisee, a religious leader in Israel, who visited Jesus by night to check out His claims. The religious teachers of the time were concerned to establish what people needed to do in order to be accepted by God. Jesus challenges this way of thinking by telling Nicodemus that he has to go back to square one and begin on a new basis. "I tell you the truth, no one can see the kingdom of God unless he is born again" (v. 3). An alternative translation of the phrase "born again" is "born from above." Our salvation (or "seeing the kingdom of God") does not depend on *our* moral and spiritual achievements, but on what God has done on our behalf.

The following verses are either a continuation of Jesus' conversation or a commentary added by the Apostle John. After reading them aloud, discuss the questions which follow.

¹⁶For God so loved the world that He gave His one and only Son, that whoever believes in Him shall not perish but have eternal life. ¹⁷For God did not send His Son into the world to condemn the world, but to save the world through Him. ¹⁸Whoever believes in Him is not condemned, but whoever does not believe stands condemned already because he has not believed in the name of God's one and only Son. ¹⁹This is the verdict: Light has come into the world, but men loved darkness instead of light because their deeds were evil. ²⁰Everyone who does evil hates the light, and will not come into the light for fear that his deeds will be exposed. ²¹But whoever lives by the truth comes into the light, so that it may be seen plainly that what he has done has been done through God."

John 3:16-21

What would you say to the person who sees the Gospel as Jesus' coming into the world to placate God's anger against sinful humankind?

How does the passage challenge the idea that people who have not heard or responded positively to the claims of Christ are simply rolling through life in spiritual neutral gear?

We usually assume that more people are afraid of the dark than of the light. Why do you think John reverses this assumption?

According to one recent public poll, most churchgoers believe that "God helps those who help themselves." They may have a point if they are implying that God expects us to accept responsibility for our actions and to use our God-given strength and intelligence to provide for our material needs and to make responsible decisions. But to what extent does that commonly accepted saying apply in the area of salvation? Does God meet us halfway, so to speak? Consider the following statements.

⁸But God demonstrates His own love for us in this: While we were still sinners, Christ died for us.

Romans 5:8

¹⁸For Christ died for sins once for all, the righteous for the unrighteous to bring you to God.

1 Peter 3:18

¹⁰This is love: not that we loved God, but that He loved us and sent His Son as an atoning sacrifice for our sins.

1 John 4:10

How do these passages apply to our attitudes toward people who live blatantly immoral lives and who seem to have no interest in the Gospel of Jesus Christ?

16

Pair off and describe to each other the most godless person you know. What especially riles you about that person? Then stop to think of something you like about him or her. Having shared together, spend 30 seconds in silence with your eyes closed imagining that person as you believe God would have him or her to be.

Now, discuss as a group: is it even justifiable to write anybody off as beyond the reach of the love of God?

Reconciled to Others

The fundamental message of the Gospel is the possibility of broken relationships being restored. The New Testament insists that being put right with God also means becoming reconciled with those who have also received forgiveness through Christ.

What are the principal reasons that people in general, or individuals you know well, have rejected or ignored the Gospel? Select three from the following list, and rank them in priority order from 1 to 3.

❏ The church's perceived irrelevance in the face of current issues
❏ The opulent lifestyle and moral scandals of TV evangelists
❏ Inconsistency in the lives of professing Christians
❏ Never heard the Gospel clearly and convincingly explained
❏ Bad experiences in a church which they have attended
❏ Insensitive and inappropriate presentations of the Gospel
❏ No sense of spiritual need
❏ Intellectual obstacles to faith
❏ Other: _____

Some barriers to belief are caused by spiritual blindness and hardness of heart. But there are other obstacles to faith which we may erect either personally or as a fellowship of professing Christians.

Paul tells the believers in Philippi to swallow their pride and

17

sort out their differences. When we are faced with the enormity of what Christ was prepared to do on our behalf, then our disagreements pale into insignificance. As a group, read the following passage, slowly and thoughtfully, with each person reading just one phrase.

⁵Your attitude should be the same as that of Christ Jesus: ⁶Who, being in the very nature God, did not consider equality with God something to be grasped, ⁷but made Himself nothing, taking the very nature of a servant, being made in human likeness. ⁸And being found in appearance as a man, He humbled Himself and became obedient to death—even death on a cross! ⁹Therefore God exalted Him to the highest place and gave Him the name that is above every name, ¹⁰that at the name of Jesus every knee should bow, in heaven and on earth and under the earth, ¹¹and every tongue confess that Jesus Christ is Lord, to the glory of God the Father.

Philippians 2:5-11

The above verses are so memorable that at the time of writing they had already become an early Christian hymn.

What relevance do you think those verses have to the task of sharing the Good News?

GROWING BY DOING

The Same Attitude as Christ
With the Philippians passage open before you, list some practical steps you could take relating to each of the following issues.

ISSUE #1: MY AVAILABILITY. Jesus had to let go of the splendor and security and immunity of heaven in order to do His Father's will (v. 6).

Sometimes nonchurchgoers complain that churchgoers are too busy with their church activities to have time for anyone else! Are we open to that criticism? The longer we are mem-

18

bers of the church, the less likely we are to have many unchurched people as our close friends. The problem is likely to be most serious among those who are church leaders or are heavily involved in running church programs.

The problem is often broader than personal availability. The church has become self-preoccupied. Some churches are like a bakery that bakes first-class bread with practically the total production being consumed on the premises by the employees of the bakery. The only outlet is a customer counter located in an alley at the rear of the bakery where a few customers come. The shop opens only a few days each month for a brief period!

During the coming week, how can you become more available to the people around you?

ISSUE #2: MY ATTITUDE. Jesus as the Son of the God had to lay aside the status and privileges of Godhead. He did not come to this earth as an heavenly visitor, putting in a brief appearance from time to time. Neither did He opt to establish Himself as a remote monarch in the comfort of a kingly palace surrounded by a royal retinue and troop of bodyguards. On the contrary, He humbled Himself and became a servant (vv. 6-7).

He was, in the first place, a servant to His Heavenly Father. He also made Himself available to the crowds who clamored for His attention. Accessibility was crucial to His mission, both in ministering to the multitudes, the sick, and in discipling the Twelve who were His constant companions.

Think over the contacts and conversations you have had with people you could influence for Christ. Did you make it easier or harder to believe in a God who is generous and forgiving?

What positive steps can you take to mend or improve relationships this week?

ISSUE #3: MY COMMITMENT LEVEL. Reflect on how far Jesus was prepared to go to make possible our salvation. He not only submitted to demanding labor and menial acts, He was totally obedient to the point of facing humiliation, enduring cruel torture, and bearing the agony of crucifixion. In addition to the physical torment, He experienced the spiritual desolation of separation from the companionship of His Heavenly Father as He took upon Himself the burden and penalty of the sins of the world. Nothing had ever broken those intimate ties for a single moment until Jesus' death on the cross.

What is the most difficult step or series of steps which you will need to take in order to effectively share your faith with the people around you?

What steps are you prepared to take in order to reach out to a wider circle of neighbors and colleagues?

GOING THE SECOND MILE

Prayer of Commitment

In view of the distance Jesus was prepared to go for you, how far are you prepared to go in order to make known His love to others? Write out a prayer of commitment to share your personal faith and communicate the Gospel in the coming weeks. Please be frank and honest in what you write! God encourages us to express what we really feel. He is not impressed by our pious promises which come to nothing.

Pray this prayer daily during the eight weeks of this study.

Points to Remember
List three points raised during the group discussions which you found to be particularly helpful.

1.

2.

3.

Concerns of Group Members
Identify some of the challenges that group members individually and the group as a whole will have to face in order to fulfill its obligation to share the Good News with a needy world.

Think through the contributions made by the other members of your group and pray for individuals in response to the concerns they expressed.

TWO

Expressing Our Gratitude

A Message Too Important to Keep to Ourselves
At the first display of generosity we find ourselves overwhelmed with gratitude toward the person who surprised us with the gift. When that generosity is repeated on a regular basis, however, we may find ourselves taking it for granted. We can even reach the point when we think that the supply is available on demand.

 ## GETTING ACQUAINTED

It's Just What I Wanted!
Can you think of an occasion when someone, either known to you or acting anonymously, surprised you with a generous gift of something which was just what you needed at that time? It may have been money for a holiday, a place to stay, furniture, or vital equipment. Tell the group about it.

"What Do You Say, Junior?"
If you are a parent, share ways in which you have tried to make sure that your children have expressed their gratitude to relatives and friends who have sent them Christmas and birthday presents.

23

Taken for Granted
Think of occasions when you felt that you had been taken for granted. Do you know people who come to you only when they want something? How do you feel about them?

GAINING INSIGHT

Motivation and Methodology
The followers of Jesus in New Testament times succeeded in spreading the Good News of sins forgiven and of the new life in Christ with remarkable speed and effectiveness. Despite the numerical strength of the contemporary church, its prestigious educational institutions, and books, films, and TV stations, we have not been able to match their performance—at least in the Western world.

Our problem is not so much in the area of methodology as in motivation, which is the concern of this session. Paul addresses this issue in the following passage from his second letter to the believers in Corinth.

Underline any word or phrase that throws light on what motivated Paul to communicate the Gospel, or that could motivate the Corinthians to share that message with others.

This passage contains some difficult verses, so don't worry if some things are not clear at the outset!

¹¹Since, then, we know what it is to fear the Lord, we try to persuade men. What we are is plain to God, and I hope it is also plain to your conscience. ¹²We are not trying to commend ourselves to you again, but are giving you an opportunity to take pride in us, so that you can answer those who take pride in what is seen rather than in what is in the heart. ¹³If we are out of our mind, it is for the sake of God; if we are in our right mind, it is for you. ¹⁴For Christ's love compels us, because we are convinced that one died for all, and therefore all died. ¹⁵And He died for all, that those who live should no longer live for themselves but for Him who died for them and was raised again.

¹⁶So from now on we regard no one from a worldly point of view. Though we once regarded Christ in this way, we do so no longer. ¹⁷Therefore, if anyone is in Christ, he is a new creation; the old has gone, the new has come! ¹⁸All this is from God, who reconciled us to Himself through Christ and gave us the ministry of reconciliation: ¹⁹that God was reconciling the world to Himself in Christ, not counting men's sins against them. And He has committed to us the message of reconciliation. ²⁰We are therefore Christ's ambassadors, as though God were making His appeal through us. We implore you on Christ's behalf: Be reconciled to God. ²¹God made Him who had no sin to be sin for us, so that in Him we might become the righteousness of God.

¹As God's fellow workers we urged you not to receive God's grace in vain. ²For He says,

"In the time of My favor I heard you,
And in the day of salvation I helped you."

I tell you, now is the time of God's favor, now is the day of salvation.

2 Corinthians 5:11–6:2

What words express the urgency Paul feels to communicate the Gospel? List below the words which you noticed in the passage and add any additional words mentioned by others in the group.

To whom did Paul feel himself to be primarily accountable (v. 11)?

The preceding verse states, **For we must all appear before the judgment seat of Christ, that each one may receive what is due him for the things done while in the body whether good or bad** (2 Corinthians 5:10). Do you think

Paul's "fear of the Lord" was terror of the prospect of being held accountable? Or do you think he is saying something else?

Paul was not simply driven by a sense of obligation; he felt an equally powerful inner constraint inspired by Christ's love (v. 14). Christ has not only demonstrated His love to us, He also desires to express His love through us to a lost world.

Study verse 15 carefully to discover the major obstacle that must be removed in order for God's people to begin to share the Good News of Christ. What are some of the ways in which believers today are spiritually sidetracked so that they live for themselves?

How can you help each other resist the strong cultural pressures to live to "look after Number One?"

In many situations the problem facing the would-be witness who is eager to share the Gospel is not only fear of rejection by friends outside the church, but of ridicule by some church members. We are not alone in this, for Paul also had his critics who tried to undermine his ministry by working behind his back to make his converts turn against him (see v. 12).

In response, Paul makes a curious statement that is worth pondering: **If we are in out of our mind, it is for the sake of God; if we are in our right mind, it is for you** (v. 13).

What do you think Paul is suggesting by "out of our mind"?

What do you think Paul means when he describes his witness

and teaching among the Corinthians as being undertaken while in his right mind?

Worship and Witness

Many of the psalms in the Old Testament establish the closest of links between worship and witness. Consider the following examples.

[14]But as for me, I will always have hope;
 I will praise You more and more.
My mouth will tell of Your righteousness,
 Of Your salvation all day long
 though I know not its measure.

Psalm 71:14-15

[1]Sing to the Lord a new song;
 sing to the Lord, all the earth.
[2]Sing to the Lord, praise His name;
 proclaim His salvation day after day.
[3]Declare His glory among the nations, His marvelous
 deeds among all peoples.

Psalm 96:1-3

[1]I will exalt You, my God the King;
 I will praise Your name for ever and ever.
[2]Every day I will praise You
 and extol Your name for ever and ever.

[3]Great is the Lord and most worthy of praise;
 His greatness no one can fathom.
[4]One generation will commend Your works to another;
 they will tell of Your mighty acts.

Psalm 145:1-4

Why do you think there is such a close connection between worship and witness? List your reasons:

27

Reconciliation and Relationships

Paul was boundlessly grateful to God for the dramatic turn-around in his own life beginning with his conversion on the Damascus road. Up until that moment he had regarded Christ from a worldly point of view (2 Corinthians 5:16). In other words, he rejected Christ's claims, as did the majority of influential Jews at the time. Paul's dramatic change of mind resulted in his changing sides and giving his allegiance to Jesus Christ. It also resulted in his viewing everyone else in a new light.

So from now on we regard no one from a worldly point of view (5:16). The *Revised English Bible* helpfully renders Paul's declaration, **With us therefore worldly standards have ceased to count in our estimate of anyone.**

What are the criteria by which people tend to be judged in our culture, and by the church subculture?

Consider the following passage from Paul's first letter to the Corinthians, which lists the kind of people to be found in the church there, and ask yourself, "Would these people be welcomed and feel comfortable in our church?"

⁹Do you not know that the wicked will not not inherit the kingdom of God? Do not be deceived: Neither the sexually immoral nor adulterers nor male prostitutes nor homosexual offenders ¹⁰nor thieves nor the greedy nor drunkards nor slanderers nor swindlers will inherit the kingdom of God. ¹¹And that is what some of you were. But you were washed, you were sanctified, you were justified in the name of the Lord Jesus Christ and by the Spirit of God.

1 Corinthians 6:9-11

How do you think these people were contacted, brought to Christ, and welcomed into the fellowship of believers in Corinth?

What illustrations of the power of the Gospel to radically transform lives have you witnessed in your church?

Are we prepared to accept people as they are, **compelled by the love of Christ?** (2 Corinthians 5:14) Do we believe in the transforming power of the Gospel?

Look at Paul's statement: **Therefore, if anyone is in Christ, he is a new creation; the old has gone, the new has come** (5:17). In place of *anyone*, think of someone you know who seems most opposed to the Gospel, and repeat Paul's declaration, substituting that person's name.

By what descriptive title does Paul call the Christian witness? (Look at 2 Corinthians 5:20.)

What qualities and skills does this title suggest to you?

The message entrusted to us must be shared clearly and concisely. In your own words explain what is the heart of the **message of reconciliation** (5:18).

What does the Gospel have to do with relationships?

 ## GROWING BY DOING

Praise God
Spend a few minutes praising God the Father, Son, and Holy Spirit for all that They have done in making salvation available to the whole world.

Express your gratitude to God for drawing you to Himself, and for the relationship which has been established since that initial reconciliation.

Tell Others
Share with one another specific ways in which God has made a significant impact on your life.

Examine Relationships
Think if there is any individual that you have discounted because you find him or her objectionable or hostile. Ask God to help you to see that person through His eyes as that person could become by the transforming power of the Gospel. Each time you encounter that person try to keep that image in mind. Pray that God will pour His love into your heart to show love and forgiveness for that person. We cannot be ambassadors of reconciliation while, at the same time, holding grudges against the very people we are meant to reach.

Identify Your Posting
Recognize each person in the group as an AMBASSADOR FOR CHRIST. Each ambassador has a posting—where God has placed us in our neighborhoods, places of work, network of friends and associates. Share with the other group members some of the situations you anticipate facing during the coming week, and describe the challenges you will face as a representative of the kingdom of God and a witness for Jesus Christ.

If appropriate, pray a prayer of commissioning so that the person is sent out by the group and with its support.

Lord, we thank You that You have commissioned _____ _____ as your special representative in _____ during the coming week.

Grant Your love, discernment, and guidance, that he/she will be a faithful witness and authentic ambassador of Your coming kingdom. This we ask in the name of Jesus Christ. Amen.

GOING THE SECOND MILE

Ministry of Reconciliation

During this session God may have been reminding you of someone against whom you hold a grudge, someone who has made you bitter, or a person you are choosing to avoid or ignore.

If so, then seek opportunity to change your attitude toward that individual or to put right an old grievance.

Christ has for you, His ambassador, some issue that He would have you address in your home or place of work. Remember that an ambassador must be as open to receive messages as to deliver them! Be open this week to the initiatives the Lord would have you take, and how you should go about the task. You might want to seek wisdom from the group if you feel that you can take them into your confidence. There's all the difference in the world between getting emotional and getting involved. We need to remind ourselves how far Jesus was prepared to go on our behalf.

²¹Christ was innocent of sin, and yet for our sake God made Him one with human sinfulness, so that in Him we might be made one with the righteousness of God.

2 Corinthians 5:21, *Revised English Bible*

THREE

Treating a Terminal Condition

Timely Interventions

Some of us have had the distressing experience of watching a friend or loved one suffering through the final stages of a terminal illness. We have felt our helplessness as we have observed its progress causing pain and progressive weakness and loss of faculties. Perhaps we have vented our anger against God because He has not intervened in response to our pleadings to arrest the progress of the disease and bring healing.

We thought, "If only the condition had been detected and treated sooner. Perhaps then it could have been successfully treated." But now it seems too late.

Sin is a terminal condition if it remains untreated. In this session we will examine the widespread influence and terrible consequences of sin, and discover how Christ's death, resurrection, and ascension provide a unique and 100 percent cure.

 GETTING ACQUAINTED

Caring for the Ill

Form groups of three or four to share with one another experiences you have had in caring for someone with a chronic or terminal illness. How did you feel? What questions troubled your mind?

Sickness and Sin
In what ways is sin comparable to a chronic and terminal illness? What can we learn from that?

Next, reflect on the important differences between sickness and sin in a person's life. Do you think:

1. All sickness is a direct consequence of sin?   YES   NO

2. No sickness is a consequence of sin?   YES   NO

3. Some sickness is a consequence of sin?   YES   NO

Discuss the reasoning behind your choice of answers.

GAINING INSIGHT
Two Kinds of Slavery
The Apostle Paul describes how sin influences a person's life with the object of taking complete possession. Paul's teaching is all the more significant in that it is addressed primarily to the believer rather than to the outsider. However, unbelievers cannot be excluded completely because there were probably people present when this letter was first read who had not yet committed their lives to Christ.

¹⁵What then? Shall we sin because we are not under law but under grace? By no means! ¹⁶Don't you know that

when you offer yourselves to someone to obey him as slaves, you are slaves to the one whom you obey—whether you are slaves to sin, which leads to death, or to obedience, which leads to righteousness? ¹⁷But thanks be to God that, though you used to be slaves to sin, you whole-heartedly obeyed the form of teaching to which you were entrusted. ¹⁸You have been set free from sin and have become slaves to righteousness.

¹⁹I put this in human terms because you are weak in your natural selves. Just as you used to offer the parts of your body in slavery to impurity and to ever-increasing wickedness, so now offer them in slavery to righteousness leading to holiness. ²⁰When you were slaves to sin, you were free from the control of righteousness. ²¹What benefit did you reap at that time from the things you are now ashamed of? Those things result in death! ²²But now that you have been set free from sin and have become slaves of God, the benefit you reap leads to holiness, and the result is eternal life. ²³For the wages of sin is death, but the gift of God is eternal life in Christ Jesus our Lord.

Romans 6:15-23

Slavery Begins (vv. 17-18)
At the outset we all have but one master. We begin life as slaves of sin (vv. 17-18). How do we escape from Satan's bondage?

What can you learn from verses 17 and 18 about the Gospel and our response to it?

How would you answer the person who claims to be born again while insisting that, because of forgiveness, it is OK to indulge in sin?

Slavery Develops (v. 19)

By his expression, "I put this in human terms," Paul is recognizing that in many ways his description of the believer's relationship to Christ in terms of slavery is both inadequate and misleading. When we think of slavery we think of injustice, cruelty, degradation, and oppression. This is quite the opposite of the believers' experience; we find ourselves overwhelmed by the love, generosity, and affirmation that Christ brings.

Paul is here drawing attention to the paradox that it is only in serving Christ that true freedom is to be found.

From verse 19, how would you describe each form of slavery?

❑ as a slave to sin

❑ as a slave of Christ

Having recognized that the term "slave" can be inappropriately applied, what do you think Paul wants to communicate by his use of the word?

Notice that each form of slavery follows a progression. Think of a well-publicized example of someone who has been exposed for moral corruption or criminal intent. What might have been some of the influences and steps which, although seemingly trivial at the beginning, led ultimately to an inescapable pattern of degenerate or criminal behavior?

Slavery's Result (vv. 20-22)

When you apply for a new job, you don't just listen to the promises made, you take a careful look at the pay and benefits being promised.

Slavery is the ultimate form of "employment." It is for life and entails the surrender of our whole being. Compare the "benefits" offered in the two forms of slavery.

As a slave of Satan we eventually get what we deserve — death. "Death" in the Bible does not simply refer to physical death, but to alienation and eternal separation from the presence of God.

Death is not simply a physical event which terminates life on earth, it is a spiritual state. People whose only concern is with created things have cut themselves off from the source of true life. Death becomes the power which is in control of their life as a present reality.

Believers are still subject to physical death, because they are part of the present created order which will one day pass away. But the death of Christ removed "the sting of death." It is no longer the point of eternal separation, but of instant reunion with the Lord.

In what way does the person who is a slave to sin get what he or she deserves?

In what way does the believer get what he or she does not deserve?

Remember that Paul addressed these words primarily to Christians. Why do you think Christians need to be reminded again of alternative ways of living?

What impact does sin in the believer's life have on the witness to those who are not yet followers of Christ?

Does our awareness of sins committed after our conversion prevent us from effective witness?

Can a person witness without first dealing with unconfessed sin?

GROWING BY DOING

Deadly Virus
Consider the following:

Imagine that you are a skilled physician. Through a research project you isolate an up-until-now undiscovered virus. As your research continues, you find to your amazement, that in all probability this virus has infected 100 percent of the human race. Indeed, every man, woman, and child from every culture on earth has contracted the disease.

As your research continues, you come to the shocking realization that this disease is also 100 percent fatal. Your thoughts are filled with the staggering implications. "This means I have the disease," you painfully realize. Visions of your family, friends, and other loved ones race through your mind. The thought of 4.5 billion people with the disease is too frightening to appreciate fully. Further research only confirms your findings. Though the symptoms may at times be almost unnoticeable and are often subtle and unalarming, though they may vary from person to person and from culture to culture, the result is the same. This virus is a killer.

After the shock of your discovery abates, your concern turns to some practical and pressing questions. Can the world bear to hear? Is there hope for a cure? You press on with your research. It would be unthinkable to break this devastating news without also announcing the good news of a cure.

Your research pays off—you find the cure. You develop a means of administering it and treat yourself as the first patient. It works! Your tests indicate the virus is destroyed. You can hardly contain your joy as you remove yourself from the terminal list. Now your thoughts turn to your family and your friends—in fact, to the entire world. There is hope! But your joy of discovery is tempered by the sober realization of the critical condition of others. Even at this moment the virus continues to take lives.

You arrange a press conference to bring the joyful news of the cure to the public. To your surprise, only a few of your colleagues and some newspeople attend. Your colleagues seem to be embarrassed for you. "What virus? A universal disease? Who, me? I feel just fine," are the only comments you hear. Even your family and friends are skeptical of the idea of a "universal, terminal disease." A few take you seriously, but mostly, you are treated with polite indifference.

(Mark McCloskey, *Tell It Often—Tell It Well,* Here's Life Publishers, 1985, pp. 11–12).

What details of this story do you think can be applied to the task of evangelism?

Describe the emotions you felt as you listened to the story . . .

❑ with regard to yourself.

❏ with regard to the people that are near and dear to you.

❏ with regard to the 4.5 billion who have had no opportunity to hear the message of salvation through Jesus Christ.

Getting Specific
Being concerned with *everywhere* must begin with *somewhere* and with specific individuals. Form groups of three, and share the names of three people for whom you feel particularly concerned.

Commit to pray for each other daily during the remaining five weeks.

GOING THE SECOND MILE

Reflection
Reflect further on the Bible passage studied in this session. Ask yourself:

❏ Have I been guilty of excusing sin in my life, on the basis that as I am "saved" it will not have serious consequences, and I can receive forgiveness at any time?

❏ What is the link between holiness and usefulness?

Openness to Opportunity
Watch for openings God is creating for you to demonstrate His love or say a word in His behalf to the three people for whom you feel special concern.

FOUR

This Is My Story

Sharing My Experience of God's Love

Many people are hesitant to share their personal testimony—those significant turning points in their lives when they became aware of God's interventions and presence to guide, protect, or give them understanding of the nature and relevance of the Gospel. What are the reasons for such reluctance?

It may be that the only testimonies that we have heard have been of the more sensational variety—how God saved me from a life of crime, or how I miraculously recovered from a terminal illness, or how I became a millionaire out of a life of poverty. Such stories may be impressive and even entertaining, but they are not the experiences with which most people readily identify.

Never underestimate the significance of your story, no matter how ordinary it may seem to you, as a means of helping another person who has no personal faith in God.

 ## GETTING ACQUAINTED

Word Association

What words immediately come to mind when the word *evangelist* is mentioned?

Who is the person who has been most influential in helping you know what God is like? What adjectives would you use to describe that person?

Compare and contrast the two lists of adjectives. What do the differences tell you about the work of witness and evangelism?

GAINING INSIGHT

Paul's Conversion

The story of the conversion of the Apostle Paul provides the classic dramatic encounter with a clear "before" and "after" — a sudden and significant change. Paul's experience was clearly important for Luke, who not only records the event in detail (see Acts 9:1-22), but also gives the substance of Paul's personal testimony before a hostile crowd in the temple (22:2-21) and before King Agrippa (26:1-29). We will base our study on Paul's words to the crowd, where he had to respond spontaneously to a hostile audience.

PHASE ONE: Paul's Preconversion Life

²Then Paul said: ³"I am a Jew, born in Tarsus of Cilicia, but brought up in this city. Under Gamaliel I was thoroughly trained in the law of our fathers and was just as zealous for God as any of you are today. ⁴I persecuted the followers of this Way to their death, arresting both men and women and throwing them into prison, ⁵as also the high priest and all the Council can testify. I even obtained letters from them to their brothers in Damascus, and went there to bring these people as prisoners to Jerusalem to be punished.

Acts 22:2-5

In what ways does Paul relate to his audience?

Paul's preconversion life prepared him for his future ministry. What did his years in Tarsus contribute?

What did he learn from Gamaliel, one of the most famous of the first-century rabbis?

Review your own birth, upbringing, and training. How have those experiences prepared you for future Christian service and witness?

How can a person be at the same time "zealous for God" and a persecutor of the followers of the Way?

Do you know anyone as antagonistic to Christianity as Saul (who later became Paul)? What encouragement does Paul's transformation bring to your own circle of contacts?

PHASE TWO: Paul's Conversion

⁶**About noon as I came near Damascus, suddenly a bright light from heaven flashed around me. ⁷I fell to the ground and heard a voice say to me, "Saul! Saul! Why do you persecute Me?"**

⁸**"Who are You, Lord?" I asked.**

"I am Jesus of Nazareth, whom you are persecuting," He replied. ⁹My companions saw the light, but they did not understand the voice of Him who was speaking to me.

¹⁰**"What shall I do, Lord?" I asked.**

"Get up," the Lord said, "and go into Damascus. There you will be told all that you have been assigned to do." ¹¹My companions led me by the hand into Damascus, because the brilliance of the light had blinded me.

45

¹²A man named Ananias came to see me. He was a devout observer of the law and highly respected by the Jews living there. ¹³He stood beside me and said, "Brother Saul, receive your sight!" And at that very moment I was able to see him.

¹⁴Then he said: "The God of our fathers has chosen you to know His will and to see the Righteous One and to hear words from His mouth. ¹⁵You will be His witness to all men of what you have seen and heard. ¹⁶And now what are you waiting for? Get up, be baptized and wash your sins away, calling on His name."

Acts 22:6–16

In the following chart, distinguish those aspects which are particular to Paul from those elements which are vital to any genuine commitment to Christ.

PARTICULAR TO PAUL	APPLICABLE TO ALL

How did your friends react when they became aware that you have experienced an encounter with the Lord?

Note Paul's two questions:

❏ Who are You, Lord?

❏ What shall I do, Lord?

46

What can we learn from Jesus' answers when people encounter God today?

Paul's dramatic encounter with Christ did not mean that he did not need the help of others. What roles did his companions and Ananias play?

At the time of your own commitment to Christ, did you have people alongside who helped you to process that experience and realize its implications? In what specific ways did they help you at that time?

If you had no such person, what help would you have appreciated?

What were the immediate steps urged by Ananias and taken by Paul to seal his commitment?

What were they in your case, and were they adequate?

PHASE THREE: Paul's Postconversion

¹⁷When I returned to Jerusalem and was praying at the temple, I fell into a trance ¹⁸and saw the Lord speaking. "Quick!" He said to me. "Leave Jerusalem immediately, because they will not accept your testimony about Me!"

¹⁹"Lord," I replied, "these men know that I went from one synagogue to another to imprison and beat those who believe in You. And when the blood of Your martyr Stephen was shed, I stood there giving my approval and guarding the clothes of those who were killing him."

²¹Then the Lord said to me, "Go; I will send you far away to the Gentiles."

Acts 22:17-21

Why did Paul encounter immediate problems in being accepted by the disciples of Christ in Jerusalem?

47

Have there been problems in your church regarding the acceptance of new believers into the fellowship? If so, what was the nature of the problems?

In your own case, did you encounter difficulty in being welcomed and incorporated into the life of the church?

Many people in the United States claim a "born-again experience," but it has had little impact on their subsequent life. Why do you think this has been the case with so many people?

Is the close link between Paul's conversion and calling to be a witness to the Gentiles confined to him as an Apostle, or does it relate to the experience of every person who is converted?

The Shepherd's Psalm
This personal testimony focuses on an ongoing personal relationship with the Lord, depicted as a protecting shepherd (Psalm 23:1-4) and a generous host (vv. 5-6).

¹The Lord is my shepherd, I shall not be in want.
²He makes me to lie down in green pastures,
    He leads me beside quiet waters,
³He restores my soul.
    He guides me in paths of righteousness for His name's sake.
⁴Even though I walk through the valley of the shadow of death,
    I will fear no evil, for You are with me;
    Your rod and staff, they comfort me.
⁵You prepare a table before me in the presence of my enemies.

You anoint my head with oil; my cup overflows.
⁶Surely goodness and love will follow me
 all the days of my life,
 and I will dwell in the house of the Lord forever.

Psalm 23

Many people feel that they do not have a testimony because they cannot point to a time and place when they had a decisive conversion experience. The crucial point is not that we have to know the date and time of our birth, simply that we are aware of being alive!

Drawing from the experience of David in this psalm, what have you learned in the course of your walk with God regarding:

❑ God's provision to meet your material needs?

❑ The need for times of rest and relaxation?

❑ The Lord's help in making difficult decisions when you were pressured or tempted to make moral compromises?

❑ God's presence through a crisis in which you did not know what to do, or from which there seemed to be no light at the end of the tunnel?

What have been some of the high points of your walk with the Lord, when you have had occasion to rejoice in God's generosity?

GROWING BY DOING

Sharing Our Stories
Pair with a member of the other group and take five minutes each to share with one another your journey of faith.

What do you have in common?

What were the significant differences in the way in which the Lord dealt with each of you?

Prayer Groups
Spend the remaining time in the prayer groups you formed last week, and remind one another of the three persons you want to see come to a saving faith in Christ. Write the names of all the people here:

GOING THE SECOND MILE

Write Your Testimony
Write out your personal testimony, confining it to a maximum of four pages. Having written it down, say it out loud at least three times.

Pray for Opportunities
Pray for at least one opportunity to share your story with another person who is not yet a believer.

Pray for People
Set aside three periods of at least 30 minutes to pray for your own three names and for the other members of your prayer group and the names of the people for whom they have asked you to pray.

FIVE

Whom Do I Know?

Starting Close to Home

We are all in the business of making introductions. Sometimes it is simply to help a person feel socially included. Or the occasion may be with a view to forging a business deal. Or linking a person looking for a job to a potential employer. At other times you might be acting as a "matchmaker" between two people of the opposite sex.

GETTING ACQUAINTED

May I Introduce . . .

Think back over the past week. Whom have you introduced to whom? Share some instances which have occurred.

Why did you make the introductions?

What was the immediate outcome?

Did you have any long-term aspirations?

The task of the evangelist can be described as making introductions between a person prepared to be found by Christ and the seeking Savior.

 GAINING INSIGHT

John Introduces Jesus
Read the following passage.

²⁹The next day John saw Jesus coming toward him and said, "Look, the Lamb of God, who takes away the sin of the world! ³⁰This is the One I meant when I said, 'A Man who comes after me has surpassed because He was before me.' ³¹I myself did not know Him, but the reason I came baptizing with water was that He might be revealed to Israel."

³²Then John gave this testimony: "I saw the Spirit come down from heaven as a dove and remain on Him. ³³I would not have known Him, except that the One who sent me to baptize with water told me, 'The Man on whom you see the Spirit come down and remain is He who will baptize with the Holy Spirit.' ³⁴I have seen and testify that this is the Son of God."

John 1:29-34

The testimony of John the Baptist provides us with our first two important lessons regarding the task of the witness.

First, the task of the witness is to point people to Jesus and not to gather a personal following. How did John do this?

Second, the witness can only testify to as much as he or she knows. We are not expected to know everything. What were the limitations in John's witness?

Having seen the Holy Spirit identify Jesus as the Messiah, did John from that point on never experience serious doubts? (See Matthew 11:2-6.)

In what ways do you feel disqualified or ill-equipped to be an effective witness?

What can you learn from the witness of John the Baptist?

Consider also the impact of two other witnesses recorded in the Gospels:

❑ The Samaritan woman who met Jesus at the well, and immediately went back into town to share her story (John 4:27-42).

❑ The demon-possessed man who, immediately after he was delivered, was ordered to return home rather than accompany Jesus and the disciples (Mark 5:18-20).

What can we learn from these accounts about the essential qualification for a person to become a witness?

Andrew Finds Cephas
Read the following passage.

³⁵The next day John was there again with two of his disciples. ³⁶When he saw Jesus passing by, he said, "Look, the Lamb of God!"

55

³⁷When the two disciples heard him say this, they followed Jesus. ³⁸Turning around, Jesus saw them following and asked,

"What do you want?"

They said, "Rabbi" (which means Teacher), "where are You staying?"

³⁹"Come," He replied, "and you will see."

So they went and saw where He was staying, and spent the day with Him. It was about the tenth hour.

⁴⁰Andrew, Simon Peter's brother, was one of the two who heard what John had said and who had followed Jesus. ⁴¹The first thing Andrew did was to find his brother Simon and tell him, "We have found the Messiah" (that is, the Christ). ⁴²And he brought him to Jesus.

Jesus looked at him and said, "You are Simon son of John. You will be called Cephas" (which, when translated, is Peter).

John 1:35-42

John the Baptist was true to his calling as a witness to Jesus. He directed two of his followers to Jesus, identifying Him as "the Lamb of God" — a title used only of Jesus and indicating Jesus as God's appointed sacrifice to atone for the sins of the world.

What aspects of Jesus' person and ministry on our behalf do you emphasize when you have occasion to speak about Him to fellow believers and non-Christians? Rate the following in order of prominence in your actual conversations.

❑ HEALER who ministered to me in physical illness or emotional distress.

❑ GUIDE who has directed my life through times of perplexity.

56

❑ COMFORTER who has consoled me during times of disappointment, bereavement, anxiety or depression.

❑ SAVIOR who has secured my forgiveness by dying for my sins.

❑ LORD who has taken charge of my life and made a significant difference.

❑ Other: _____

_____

This leads us to our third point: Our witness must emphasize the uniqueness of Jesus Christ as the Son of God and Savior of the world.

Why do you think that Andrew and the unnamed disciple followed Jesus in order to discover where He lived? How does your answer apply to the contemporary person who is searching for Christ?

Where did you first find Christ or become acutely aware of His presence?

Before you are likely to be motivated to introduce a friend to Christ, what must you have done? Discuss the implications of verse 39.

Why is it inappropriate to be selfish or jealous in our relationship with Christ?

If you had been Andrew, can you imagine any reasons which might have kept you from wanting to share your discovery with your brother Cephas?

Last week we thought about the change that the Gospel made in the life of Saul, converting him from a persecutor of Christians into a preacher of Christ. The Lord gave Saul a new name, and here Simon is also given a new name. Why do you think the Lord did this in the case of selected individuals?

Philip Finds Nathanael
Read the following passage:

⁴³**The next day Jesus decided to leave Galilee. Finding Philip, He said to him, "Follow Me."**

⁴⁴**Philip, like Andrew and Peter, was from the town of Bethsaida. ⁴⁵Philip found Nathanael and told him, "We have found the One Moses wrote about in the Law, and about whom the prophets also wrote—Jesus of Nazareth, the son of Joseph."**

⁴⁶**"Nazareth! Can any good come from there?" Nathanael asked.**

"Come and see," said Philip.

⁴⁷**When Jesus saw Nathanael approaching, He said of him, "Here is a true Israelite, in whom there is nothing false."**

58

⁴⁸"How do You know me?" Nathanael asked.

Jesus answered, "I saw you while you were still under the fig tree before Philip called you."

⁴⁹Then Nathanael declared, "Rabbi, You are the Son of God; You are the King of Israel."

⁵⁰Jesus said, "You believe because I told you I saw you under the fig tree. You shall see greater things than that." ⁵¹He then added, "I tell you the truth, you shall see heaven open, and the angels of God ascending and descending on the Son of Man."

John 1:43-51

Sometimes, as in the case of Andrew and John, it seems at the time that we are required to take the initiative, although in retrospect we often become aware of the Lord's guiding hand. Others are suddenly confronted by the call of Christ, as was Philip. By whatever means we met Christ, it is still our responsibility to introduce others to Christ. In order to do that we must have a clear understanding as to how others can find Him. The witness personally accompanies the seeker — not, "Go and find out for yourself," but, "Come and see" (vv. 39, 46).

How does this observation apply to your personal witness and to this small group acting as a "community of witnesses"?

Andrew thought he was introducing Nathanael as someone previously unknown to Jesus. What did Jesus already know about him? How much do you think that Jesus already knows about the persons you are wanting to introduce to Him? How should that realization encourage us in our witness?

GROWING BY DOING

Reflection

Gather into the prayer groups in which you have been meeting for the previous two sessions. Share what your study of the disciples' examples of witnessing has taught you about the people you want to introduce to Jesus Christ. Reflect on each other's experiences.

Role Play

Still in your prayer group, provide a description of one of the three persons for whom you are praying regularly as a group and ask the others in your subgroup to play the role of that person as they listen to your journey of faith.

After the presentation, have each person offer his or her response to the following issues:

❑ Was the starting point appropriate?

❑ Was the language intelligible?

❑ Did the testimony have cohesion?

❑ Did it focus on Jesus Christ?

❑ Was the general content relevant to the life-situation of the person being addressed?

❑ Was it likely to generate further questions?

❑ Did it leave a positive impression?

Conclude the meeting of the subgroups by spending time in prayer for each other and the nine non-Christians for whom you have covenanted to pray.

GOING FOR THE SECOND MILE

Rewrite Your Testimony

Rewrite your testimony, incorporating any comments from the subgroup which were particularly helpful, and bearing in mind the guidelines listed below.

PREPARING YOUR TESTIMONY

1. Begin with an introductory paragraph describing the person for whom your presentation is intended, and ask yourself, as you work through your presentation, whether it is appropriate for that individual.

2. Keep the length to within four sides, double-space if typed.

3. Emphasize the *why* and *how* you become a Christian and the difference that commitment has made, rather than the *when* and *where*, unless they are a point of contact with the recipient.

4. Express in one sentence the main point which you want to get across in your faith story. What Gospel truth above all else does the person need to hear from your experience of the grace of God?

5. Select two or three illustrations from your life which relate to the main thrust of your presentation.

6. Ensure that you are not using any religious jargon or technical theological vocabulary and that you are not making passing references to the Bible on the misguided assumption that the recipient has the necessary background knowledge to understand what you are saying.

7. Check through your first draft to edit out anything which is couched in religious jargon, is irrelevant, or is vague or dishonest.

8. Read it aloud to yourself at least three times. Does it sound "natural"? Do you feel comfortable saying it? Then repeat it from memory. You don't have to be word perfect.

61

9. Share it with some Christian friends. It will encourage them and help build your confidence.

10. Think of how your story might be told from alternative angles so that it will make an impact on other non-Christians with whom you are in contact. This will help you to avoid becoming stereotyped in your presentation and help prepare you to respond to a wider range of witnessing opportunities.

Get Feedback

Ask a friend who is not yet a Christian if he or she will read through what you have written, explaining that it is an assignment for a course you are doing at church on putting your faith into words. Say you would welcome any comments as to whether what you have written is clear and is a true description of what they know about you. This is not an evangelistic ploy, but a genuine desire for feedback!

Keep Praying

Continue to pray three times a week for the other members of your subgroup and for the nine people who are not yet believers, assigning at least 30 minutes for each time of prayer. Thank God for what He is already beginning to do in the lives of these persons.

SIX

Taking Time

Balancing Urgency with Patience

When making a major decision in life, such as choosing a partner in marriage, or deciding on a career, or considering whether or not to emigrate to another country, most of us want time to consider the pros and cons and to gather as much information as possible. We would probably caution people from making a premature decision on the basis of an emotional whim or hunch, without stopping to face the facts.

Despite our sense of urgency as we tell others the Good News of salvation, we need to allow people to consider seriously the commitment involved.

 ## GETTING ACQUAINTED

Meeting Mr./Ms. Right

How did you meet your spouse, or how did your parents or other close family members meet their partners?

What do different stories shared in the group tell you of the variety of ways in which relationships develop?

GAINING INSIGHT

No Hard Sell

I overheard a passenger on a plane journey comment to a fellow passenger about the Billy Graham evangelistic crusade meeting he had attended the previous night, "He didn't try and persuade me to do something which I didn't want to do." Therein lies the gift of the true evangelist.

Jesus knew that some people need to be allowed time before they are ready to come to a decision. When He talked with Nicodemus, He addressed the basic issue and gave a direct challenge, but then He appeared to back off, giving Nicodemus the opportunity and permission to go away and think over what he had heard. Jesus did not attempt to force him into a premature decision.

¹Now there was a man of the Pharisees named Nicodemus, a member of the Jewish ruling council. ²He came to Jesus at night and said, "Rabbi, we know You are a teacher who has come from God. For no one can perform the miraculous signs You are doing if God were not with him."

³In reply Jesus declared, "I tell you the truth, no one can see the kingdom of God unless he is born again."

⁴"How can a man be born when he is old?" Nicodemus asked. "Surely he cannot enter a second time into his mother's womb to be born!"

⁵Jesus answered, "I tell you the truth, no one can enter the kingdom of God unless he is born of water and the Spirit. ⁶Flesh gives birth to flesh, but the Spirit gives birth to spirit. ⁷You should not be surprised at My saying, 'You must be

born again.' ⁸The wind blows wherever it pleases, You hear its sound, but you cannot tell where it comes from or where it is going. So it is with everyone born of the Spirit."

⁹"How can this be?" Nicodemus asked.

¹⁰"You are Israel's teacher," said Jesus, "and do you not understand these things? ¹¹I tell you the truth, we speak of what we know, and we testify to what we have seen, but still you people do not accept our testimony. ¹²I have spoken to you of earthly things and you do not believe; how then will you believe if I speak of heavenly things? ¹³No one has ever gone into heaven except the One who came from heaven—the Son of Man. ¹⁴Just as Moses lifted up the snake in the desert, so the Son of Man must be lifted up, ¹⁵that everyone who believes in Him may have eternal life."

John 3:1-15

Nicodemus opened the conversation by stating his convictions about Jesus. He seemed to be expressing a consensus of the views of fellow council members as well as the population at large.

Summarize the opinions about Jesus that would be typical of the people with whom you are in contact outside of the church context.

How do your findings relate to your presentation of the Gospel?

Why do you think Jesus immediately spoke to Nicodemus in terms of the kingdom of God? What is the relationship between Nicodemus' opening statement and Jesus' response?

Born-Again Christians

The term "born again" triggers contrasting responses. To some it is a badge of religious orthodoxy, while to others it smacks of religious presumption and superficiality.

According to market-researcher George Barna:

❑ One-third of all adults (34%) classify themselves as born-again Christians.

❑ The people most likely to view themselves as born-again Christians are those 45 or older (i.e., pre-Boomers); those who have not graduated from college; and individuals whose household incomes are below $60,000.

❑ Blacks (55%) are more likely than whites (32%) to accept this label.

❑ Among those who call themselves born-again Christians, only 65% actually believe that they will have eternal life because they have confessed their sins and have accepted Jesus Christ as their Savior.

❑ Two-thirds of those who attend evangelical churches (69%) state that they are born again. Half as many (32%) who attend mainline Protestant churches claim to be born again. Among Catholics, 14% say they are born again.

(Source: George Barna, *What Americans Believe*, Ventura, CA: Regal Books, 1991, p. 179.)

What do these findings suggest to you about our use of the phrase in the contemporary North American context?

Write out your own definition of the term and share it with the rest of your group.

❏ Definition of the term *born again:*

Why do you think Jesus told Nicodemus, who was a sincerely religious person and knowledgable in the Scriptures that he had to start all over again on an entirely different basis?

What religious obstacles would he have to face?

What social barriers would he have to surmount?

How would you seek to help a churchgoer who was depending on religion, family upbringing, inherited beliefs, and good works to earn salvation?

What do you think Jesus wanted Nicodemus to understand by His statement, "No one can enter the kingdom of God unless he is born of water and the Spirit?" (v. 5)

❏ WATER symbolizes . . .

❏ SPIRIT represents . . .

In light of the above, how would you now define the term "born again?" Note that it can equally be described as "born from above."

It is clear from Jesus' conversation that being born again is both supernatural (v. 6, compare 1:12, 13) and unpredictable (v. 8). What are the practical implications of these two insights for your current evangelistic concerns?

❏ Because the new birth is SUPERNATURAL, I must . . .

❏ Because the new birth is UNPREDICTABLE, I must . . .

How have these two features been evident in your own relationship with the Lord?

Look and Live
At the conclusion of John's account of the interview, Jesus draws Nicodemus back to his opening statement, "Rabbi, we know You are a teacher come from heaven." Jesus now proceeds to show the limitations in what Nicodemus knows.

Earlier Jesus had emphasized the point, "You must be born again." Now He teaches Nicodemus that the new birth is made possible through a vital relationship with the Son of Man, who is also the only Son of God whom the Father has sent from heaven on a divine mission.

Jesus emphasizes His point by referring to an incident that occurred while Israel was about to enter Canaan after wandering through the Sinai desert under the leadership of Moses.

70

Read the account.

⁴They traveled from Mount Hor along the route to the Red Sea, to go around Edom. But the people grew impatient on the way; ⁵they spoke against God and against Moses, and said, "Why have you brought us up out of Egypt to die in the desert? There is no bread! There is no water! And we detest this miserable food!"

⁶Then the Lord sent venomous snakes among them; they bit the people and many Israelites died. ⁷The people came to Moses and said, "We sinned when we spoke against the Lord and against you. Pray that the Lord will take the snakes away from us." So Moses prayed for the people.

⁸The Lord said to Moses, "Make a snake and put it up on a pole; anyone who is bitten can look at it and live." ⁹So Moses made a bronze snake and put it up on a pole. Then when anyone was bitten by a snake and looked at the bronze snake, he lived.

Numbers 21:4-9

Why do you think Jesus alluded to this incident? What similarities do you see in the attitudes of the people of Moses' day and Jesus' day? What was their only hope of escaping the consequences of their rebellion?

Notice that, although Jesus told Nicodemus that he *must* be born again, He did not insist on his making a decision there and then. In fact it is unclear at what point the interview concluded. It seems that John intentionally left it open-ended.

On two other occasions Nicodemus is mentioned briefly, and each incident is significant. John 7:50 shows him at a meeting of the Jerusalem Council insisting that Jesus be given a fair hearing. Nicodemus was prepared to speak up for Jesus, evidence that the conversation we have been studying made a lasting impression.

71

Then in John 19:38-42 we find Nicodemus accompanying Joseph of Arimathea, who is described as a secret disciple, to request from Pilate the body of Jesus. They take the body of Jesus down from the cross to place it in Joseph's own tomb. It was Nicodemus who provided the expensive spices. Why do you think that he was prepared to get involved at this time?

GROWING BY DOING

Fruitful Believers

There is urgency behind Jesus words, "You must be born again." To be a born-again believer is not a party label or a description of a certain kind of Christian. Neither does it describe an elite corpse—the Green Berets of the army of Christ. Rather it is an entrance requirement for the kingdom of God.

Galatians 5:22-23 lists the character traits which the born-again believer should grow to exemplify. Meditate on each of the words in relation to your witness and evangelism.

²²But the fruit of the Spirit is love, joy, peace, patience, kindness, goodness, faithfulness, ²³gentleness and self-control.

Galatians 5:22-23

Express some one-sentence prayers on the themes of love, joy, peace, patience, kindness, goodness, faithfulness, gentleness and self-control.

Prayer Groups

In your prayer group, share how you would explain the term *born again* to one of the three persons for whom each of you is praying, in language that would be meaningful to them.

How will you "keep the door open" with those people with whom you are seeking to share the Gospel? Are you prepared not to see an immediate response, and yet to go on believing that the Lord is at work in that person's life? What should you be doing in the meantime?

Spend time in your prayer group updating one another on the persons for whom you are praying. Then praise the Lord for any witnessing opportunities which He has given you, and pray for the needs of those individuals.

GOING THE SECOND MILE

Scripture Memory
Commit the following verses to memory:

¹²Yet to all who received Him, to those who believed in His name, He gave the right to become children of God— ¹³children born not of natural descent, nor of human decision or a husband's will, but born of God.

John 1:12-13

Outreach Events
Think how your study group might develop a long-term strategy to share the Gospel with your mutual friends through a series of planned events. Take your suggestion for the group to consider at your next session.

SEVEN

Cross Talk

Ways to Present the Gospel

It is easy to spot first-time flyers on an aircraft. They haven't heard the safety instructions before, so they dutifully watch the video, demonstrating the life jackets and oxygen masks, and they read the card provided in the seat pocket displaying the emergency exits. Despite the exhortations of the crew, the regular flyers ignore what is going on, remaining absorbed in their reading and conversation. The problem is that they have heard it all before so many times.

Sadly, many people feel the same way about the Gospel. They think they have heard it all before and consequently tune out. Yet, unlike the aircraft safety announcement, the Gospel is not communicated in the New Testament in a standard presentation, but is approached in a refreshing variety of ways. While the basic content remains the same.

The word "Gospel" literally means Good News. More specifically, it is the Good News announcing what God has accomplished on our behalf through His Son Jesus Christ. The focal point of that message is what Jesus accomplished by His death on the cross, His resurrection from the tomb, and His ascension to His Father's right hand in heaven. The Gospel has not been truly proclaimed unless those great events have been announced, explained, and applied.

GETTING ACQUAINTED

Sales Talk

Think of the last time you went to a store to make a major purchase — something that was costly, that you would be using a great deal, and that had to perform according to specifications and prove reliable. Perhaps you did not have sufficient technical knowledge to guide you in choosing between alternative models, so you asked the salesperson for an explanation of the differences, and the merits of one compared to another.

What kind of salesperson most impressed you in terms of personality, expertise, and degree of persuasiveness?

How was your experience in the store like the task of sharing the Gospel?

GAINING INSIGHT

Near and Far

Our starting points and angle of approach as we present the Gospel will depend on our audience. In the New Testament, the Gospel is presented both to those who are far away and to those who are near (Ephesians 2:17), referring respectively to Gentiles and to Jews. The Jews had a great deal of background knowledge from the Old Testament Scriptures and from God's dealing with them over the centuries as a special people, whereas the Gentiles had little or no prior knowledge.

It is much the same today. Some people we approach may have been brought up in the church, have been taught the Scriptures in childhood, and even made a "commitment to Christ" at Sunday School or youth camp, yet they still have

76

no ongoing, personal relationship with Christ. They have no assurance of salvation. They have not submitted their lives to Christ as their Lord. Or they may subsequently have rejected Christ.

"Insider" Conversion

Read this passage to see how Paul would present the Gospel to a church-related individual.

¹⁵We who are Jews by birth and not "Gentile sinners" ¹⁶know that a man is not justified by observing the law, but by faith in Jesus Christ. So we, too, have put our faith in Christ Jesus that we may be justified by faith in Christ and not by observing the law, because by observing the law no one can be justified.

¹⁷If, while we seek to be justified in Christ, it becomes evident that we ourselves are sinners, does that mean that Christ promotes sin? Absolutely not! ¹⁸If I rebuild what I destroyed, I prove that I am a lawbreaker. ¹⁹For through the law I died to the law so that I might live to God. ²⁰I have been crucified with Christ and I no longer live, but Christ lives in me. The life I live in the body, I live by faith in the Son of God, who loved me and gave Himself for me. ²¹I do not set aside the grace of God, for if righteousness could be gained through the law, Christ died for nothing!
Galatians 2:15-21

In this passage Paul alerts Peter to the fact that if the Jewish pressure group have their way, the Gospel will be undermined by legalism. Nothing must be allowed to divert us from the message of salvation by grace through faith in Christ.

In the contemporary situation, what do you consider are the major obstacles that keep people who consider themselves to be church members, or who call themselves Christians on the basis of their ethical standards, from a saving knowledge of Jesus Christ?

What example had Paul established by the response he made as someone who was himself a zealous Jew?

How did he respond to the counter argument that people who claim to have a saving knowledge of Jesus Christ can then break the law because they can count on God to continue to forgive them?

How did he respond to the charge that it is a dangerous spiritual presumption to claim to be saved?

"Outsider" Conversion

Read this passage to see how Paul would present the Gospel to a person who has never been actively involved in a local church.

¹As for you, you were dead in your transgressions and sins, ²in which you used to live when you followed the ways of this world and of the ruler of the kingdom of the air, the spirit who is now at work in those who are disobedient. ³All of us lived among them at one time, gratifying the cravings of our sinful nature and following its desires and thoughts. Like the rest, we were by nature objects of wrath. ⁴But because of His great love for us, God, who is rich in mercy, made us alive with Christ even when we were dead in transgressions—it is by grace you have been saved. ⁶And God raised us up with Christ and seated us with Him in the heavenly realms in Christ Jesus, ⁷in order that in the coming ages He might show the incomparable riches of His grace, expressed in His kindness to us in Christ Jesus. ⁸For it is by grace you have been saved, through faith—and this is not from yourselves, it is the gift of God—not by works, so that no one can boast. ¹⁰For we are God's workmanship, created in Christ Jesus to do good works, which God prepared in advance for us to do.

Ephesians 2:1-10

The church in Ephesus was predominantly Gentile, and Ephesus was a center of idolatrous worship. Although the above passage relates to Jews as well as Gentiles, for all, without exception are "dead in trespasses and sins," it was particularly applicable to Paul's Gentile readership.

How does Paul describe his hearers? (vv. 1-3)

How does this description apply to people who follow contemporary trends in society?

What is God's attitude toward those who live in this way? (See verse 3b.)

In what way does God dramatically intervene to rescue people from their spiritual bondage? List the descriptive terms in verses 5-7.

What motivated God to intervene on our behalf? (v. 9)

How does Paul describe the relationship between grace, faith, and good works in verses 8 through 10?

GROWING BY DOING

Cross Talk Guidelines

Work together on two presentations of the Gospel: one for a person with a church background and a basic knowledge of the Gospel, and the other for a secular person who was not brought up in the church and has had minimal contact.

Base each presentation on just one Bible passage, using these guidelines:

❑ Think out an appropriate introduction.

❑ Explain the passage you have chosen, using no theological terminology or religious jargon.

❑ Apply the message to the person.

Presentation to a "Churched" Person
For the person with a church-related background who is trusting in religion and morality for salvation, consider using this passage:

²²There is no difference, ²³for all have sinned and fall short of the glory of God, ²⁴and are justified freely by His grace through the redemption that came by Christ Jesus.
Romans 3:22-24

Write out a paraphrase of the above verse providing explanatory phrases for the terms "sin," "glory," "justified," and "redemption."

Using the information you have gathered from your discussion of Romans 3:23-24, discuss the following points using the diagram below:

❑ How are PEOPLE described?

❑ How is GOD described?

❑ What is the only way to cross the chasm which separates a person from God?

80

❑ Ask the individual to mark the position where he or she feels located right now.

Describe the kind of person for whom the approach taken by these verses would be particularly relevant.

Additional Scriptures: Isaiah 59:2; Ephesians 2:13.

Presentation to a Secularized Person
For the person who is depending on selfish ambition to bring fulfillment in life, consider using this passage:

¹⁵And He [Christ] died for all, that those who live should no longer live for themselves but for Him who died for them and was raised again.

¹⁶So from now on we regard no one from a worldly point of view. Though we once regarded Christ in this way, we do so no longer. ¹⁷Therefore, if anyone is in Christ, he is a new creation; the old has gone, the new has come! ¹⁸All this is from God, who reconciled us to Himself through Christ and gave us the ministry of reconciliation; ¹⁹that God was reconciling the world to Himself in Christ, not counting men's sins against them. And He has committed to us the message of reconciliation.

2 Corinthians 5:15-19

Consider the two ways of living described here. In the chart provided write out the LIFE GOALS which would represent these options.

81

SELF-CENTERED PERSON'S LIFE GOALS	CHRIST-CENTERED PERSON'S LIFE GOALS

Additional Scriptures: Matthew 16:26; Luke 9:23.

GOING THE SECOND MILE

Witnessing Tool

Obtain copies of the Gospel booklet entitled "Steps to Peace with God" to use as a regular witnessing tool. You can either read it through with someone or give it to the person at the conclusion of a conversation for him or her to think over.

The booklet can be purchased from your local Christian bookstore or ordered direct from the Billy Graham Evangelistic Association, P.O. Box 779, Minneapolis, Minnesota 55440–0779.

Scripture Helps

Learn the following verses, which will help you to bring help, challenge, and comfort to people with a variety of needs. Develop a brief presentation of the Gospel based on each passage.

❑ Lonely People—who need to meet with the Friend who will never leave or forsake them: John 10:27-29.

❑ Fearful and Apprehensive People—who need to find peace: John 14:1-4.

❑ Guilt-ridden People—who need to receive forgiveness: Psalm 103:8-14; 1 John 1:8-9.

EIGHT

It Takes a Community to Communicate

The Impact of Corporate Witness

Imagine trying to explain your favorite sport to someone who has never seen the game played. How do you explain the complex rules, the skills which must be mastered by the players, the strategies adopted, the interconnecting of skills to form a cohesive team out of a group of aggressive individuals? The more detailed your explanations, the more uninterested the person with whom you want to share your enthusiasm for the game is likely to become.

A more promising approach is to take your friend to watch a game and to be alongside to explain what is going on and answer his or her questions. Even better would be to be able to meet the team, and to be invited to their practice sessions where the professionals can give the inquirer the benefit of their experience.

It is the same combination of demonstration and explanation that is the key to effective evangelism. Just as no single professional athlete is a perfect performer, so the evangelist points to a way of life which he or she imperfectly lives out. But, as inquirers and committed Christians explore together the challenges of living "under new management" as Christ's representatives in a needy world, they help one another.

In the film *My Fair Lady,* Eliza Doolittle is a London working girl with a broad cockney accent. An aristocratic gentleman tries to teach her social refinements and provide her with elocution lessons to speak English properly. Frustrated by her slow progress, she blurts out that she's sick of words; she wants to be *shown.*

The Christian community has to be seen living out its faith in the marketplace and neighborhood—not simply as isolated individuals, but as communities of witness. It takes a community to communicate!

GETTING ACQUAINTED

Under the Influence
Think of the people who have recently influenced you to make a significant decision. They may have persuaded you to take up a sport, join a fitness club, enlist in a weight-watchers' program, change your job, go some place on vacation. Share with others in the group how that happened:

❑ Was it the recommendation of an individual or a group?

❑ How many times did they talk to you about that particular issue and over what period of time?

❑ Did you simply accept their word, or was there some evident benefit from their own experiences which influenced your decision?

❑ After making your decision, did you keep it to yourself, or have you shared your experience with others in such a way that they have either envied you or followed your example?

86

GAINING INSIGHT

Community in Small Groups

The early Christians' experience of God and the quality of their communal life aroused the curiosity of the people with whom they came into contact. The following two Bible passages provide some helpful insights into the strength of Christian community and its relation to effective evangelism.

On the day of Pentecost the believers had an overwhelming experience of God as He visited them by His Spirit with accompanying signs of a gale-force wind, flames of fire, and a supernatural communication gift of speaking in languages which they had not previously learned.

God comes to us in a variety of ways. How and when is His prerogative. The important point for our study is that the Lord gave His power to a community that had spent time deepening its relationship with Him (Acts 1:4b, 5, 14), and the Spirit came both corporately (all were included; 2:2) and individually (2:3). Together they ventured out from the security of their lodgings into the streets of Jerusalem to declare the wonders of God in the languages of the home-countries of the pilgrims gathered for the festival of Pentecost.

What explanation did Peter give to the crowd? He described the phenomenon as a fulfillment of the prophecy of Joel. He could have quoted one of the major prophets like Isaiah, Jeremiah, or Ezekiel, all of whom spoke of God imparting His Spirit to bring about a change of heart. But instead Peter chose Joel, one of the minor prophets who specifically tied the pouring out of the Spirit to prophecy.

Evangelism is a prophetic ministry in the sense that it is God speaking His saving message through His chosen servants into a specific situation to a particular group of individuals.

As an immediate result of Peter's sermon on that occasion, 3,000 persons were added to the existing community of believers that day. Just as significant is the fact that those new converts were incorporated into small groups, which in turn become operational centers for continuing outreach (v. 47).

Read aloud together the following description of the small groups which served as both centers of fellowship and witness.

⁴²They devoted themselves to the apostles' teaching and to the fellowship, to the breaking of bread and to prayer. ⁴³Everyone was filled with awe, and many wonders and miraculous signs were done by the apostles. ⁴⁴All the believers were together and had everything in common. ⁴⁵Selling their possessions and goods, they gave to anyone as he had need. ⁴⁶Every day they continued to meet together in the temple courts. They broke bread in their homes and ate together with glad and sincere hearts, ⁴⁷praising God and enjoying the favor of all the people. And the Lord added to their number daily those who were being saved.

Acts 2:42-47

Imagine that you are a new believer invited to one of the groups described in this Bible passage. Which of the activities listed might have impressed, challenged, or helped you as you began your new life as a follower of Christ?

Share your experience with small groups. What was the range and balance of their activities?

	None				Strong
TEACHING	1	2	3	4	5
FELLOWSHIP	1	2	3	4	5
PRAYER	1	2	3	4	5
PRACTICAL HELP	1	2	3	4	5
OUTREACH	1	2	3	4	5

Have you had any experience in a small group which majored on evangelism, or had it as an ongoing concern? If so, describe it to the group.

In your opinion, what is the relative importance of evangelism by small groups as against evangelistic church services, crusades, and one-on-one evangelism?

Consider the implication for evangelism of the following quotation from Howard Snyder *(Liberating the Church,* Inter-Varsity Press, 1983, p. 115).

Until recent decades, Christians could assume that when a person became a Christian or came up through a Christian family that his or her basic values were at least compatible with Christian beliefs. Because of this, it wasn't as crucial that the church lacked a real basis in community. A church without a genuine experience of community could at least function as a Christian church with some degree of integrity because society's values reinforced and overlapped those of the church.

No more. Christian consensus is gone. A person growing up in North America today simply does not have either a Christian worldview or set of values instilled by the culture. And a person entering the church from such a background begins almost at point zero in Christian life and understanding.

Outreach through Small Groups
A problem among church-related small groups is their tendency to become introverted. This is in contrast to the group life of the New Testament churches.

The aged Apostle John reflected upon his years of ministry in the following verses.

¹That which was from the beginning, which we have heard, which we have seen with our eyes, which we have looked at and our hands have touched—this we proclaim concerning the Word of life. ²The life appeared, we have seen it and testify to it, and we proclaim to you the eternal life, which was with the Father and has appeared to us. ³We proclaim to you what we have seen and heard, so that you also may have fellowship with us. And our fellowship is with the Father and with His Son, Jesus Christ. ⁴We write this to make our joy complete.

1 John 1:1-4

Notice John's corporate emphasis. He speaks in terms of "we" and "our," not "I" and "my."

What is it that the early church was so eager to proclaim?

Relate verse 1 to your own Christian experience.

❑ What have you HEARD?

❑ What have you SEEN?

❑ What have you TOUCHED? (What tangible evidence can you point to?)

What are the two vital elements of Christian fellowship as described in verse 3?

"that _____ also may have fellowship _____
_____.
And our fellowship is _____
_____ and _____,
_____."

Some small groups and home churches remind themselves of their obligation to reach out to others by placing an empty church in their circle.

The proclamation of the Gospel must be coupled with an invitation not only to respond to Christ but also to be welcomed into our fellowship.

GROWING BY DOING

Look Ahead
Plan to invite the persons for whom you have been praying in your prayer triplets to accompany you to an evangelistic church service or other church-sponsored event where there will be an opportunity to hear the Gospel during the coming three months. Write down when you will ask your friends and to what event.

Meet in your prayer group to share any opportunities God has given for witness since the previous meeting.

Look Back
Come together for a time of group sharing of what the course has meant to you in terms of your understanding and practice of evangelism.

GOING THE SECOND MILE

Plan an Outreach Meeting
Plan a further group meeting especially for evangelistic outreach among the people for whom you have been praying. Decide what would be the most appropriate format. Here are some program suggestions:

❑ A speaker who will explain how faith in Christ has impacted his or her life, followed by opportunities for others in

91

the group to add their stories and for questions to be raised.

❏ A brief presentation of the Gospel followed by people telling how that message has impacted their life.

❏ A study on a passage from one of the Gospels that focuses on the life and teaching of Jesus. Photocopy the Bible passage and ask the believers to leave their Bibles at home to ensure that everyone focuses on the one passage. Raise open-ended questions in order to allow the text to guide the discussion.

Sample questions:
What did you like about the passage?
What didn't you like about the passage?
What didn't you understand?
What helpful phrase or thought can you take with you?
What are you going to do about it?

DEAR SMALL GROUP LEADER:

Picture Yourself As A Leader.

List some words that describe what would excite you or scare you as a leader of your small group.

A Leader Is Not...
- ☐ a person with all the answers.
- ☐ responsible for everyone having a good time.
- ☐ someone who does all the talking.
- ☐ likely to do everything perfectly.

A Leader Is...
- ☐ someone who encourages and enables group members to discover insights and build relationships.
- ☐ a person who helps others meet their goals, enabling the group to fulfill its purpose.
- ☐ a protector to keep members from being attacked or taken advantage of.
- ☐ the person who structures group time and plans ahead.
- ☐ the facilitator who stimulates relationships and participation by asking questions.
- ☐ an affirmer, encourager, challenger.

❏ enthusiastic about the small group, about God's Word, and about discovering and growing.

What Is Important To Small Group Members?
❏ A leader who cares about them.
❏ Building relationships with other members.
❏ Seeing themselves grow.
❏ Belonging and having a place in the group.
❏ Feeling safe while being challenged.
❏ Having their reasons for joining a group fulfilled.

What Do You Do . . .

If nobody talks—
❏ Wait—show the group members you expect them to answer.
❏ Rephrase a question—give them time to think.
❏ Divide into subgroups so all participate.

If somebody talks too much—
❏ Avoid eye contact with him or her.
❏ Sit beside the person next time. It will be harder for him or her to talk sitting by the leader.
❏ Suggest, "Let's hear from someone else."
❏ Interrupt with, "Great! Anybody else?"

If people don't know the Bible—
❏ Print out the passage in the same translation and hand it out to save time searching for a passage.
❏ Use the same Bible versions and give page numbers.
❏ Ask enablers to sit next to those who may need encouragement in sharing.
❏ Begin using this book to teach them how to study; affirm their efforts.

If you have a difficult individual—
❏ Take control to protect the group, but recognize that exploring differences can be a learning experience.
❏ Sit next to that person.
❏ To avoid getting sidetracked or to protect another group member, you may need to interrupt, saying, "Not all of us feel that way."
❏ Pray for that person before the group meeting.

ONE

What Price?

As the **Group Leader** of this small group experience, *you* have a choice as to which elements will best fit your group, your style of leadership, and your purposes. After you examine the **Session Objectives**, select activities under each heading.

SESSION OBJECTIVES

√ To get acquainted and feel at ease in sharing naturally and spontaneously with the group.

√ To begin to relate Bible passages to our own experiences or aspirations in sharing our faith.

√ To appreciate that the Gospel is not just for respectable, religiously minded people, but is the power of God for the salvation of even the most unlikely individuals.

√ To identify some of the specific barriers to belief in the Gospel.

√ To recognize that we believers have to work on our relationships with one another if we are to communicate the Good News of reconciliation in a divided world.

GETTING ACQUAINTED 20–25 minutes

If your group is not well acquainted, take time at least to get to know one another's names before beginning this session.

Have a group member read aloud **How Far God Was Willing to Go on My Behalf.** Then use one or more of the following activities to help create a comfortable, nonthreatening atmosphere for the first meeting of your small group.

Optional—News Stories
Before this first session, scan newspapers for an article on personal heroism. Or tape a dramatic rescue story from the TV news. Use the story to introduce the concept of a brave rescue attempted at great personal sacrifice.

Personal Involvement
Invite group members to talk about any experiences they have had fighting for a cause.

Thrills and Chills
Read this section aloud, then set a tone of openness by sharing your own emotions regarding witnessing, elaborating briefly on your fears and hopes for personal evangelism. Go around the circle and let each group member tell which emotions he or she checked off, and why.

At the conclusion of the time of sharing, remind the group that the Apostle Paul was effective as a sharer of the Good News for at least three reasons. He was able to explain it clearly and comprehensively. His way of life was consistent with his message and served as a powerful reinforcement. He was deeply concerned for the persons with whom he shared the Good News.

Pocket Principle

1 To be effective in one-on-one evangelism, a person must be willing to share something of his own life. The giving of the Gospel involves the giving of oneself.

Draw the group's attention to 1 Thessalonians 2:8: "We loved you so much that we were delighted to share with you not only the Gospel but our lives as well."

GAINING INSIGHT   30–35 minutes

Reconciled to God

Nicodemus, a pillar of the religious establishment, came to check Jesus out, either on his own behalf, or on behalf of the Jewish Council. In so doing, he found himself personally challenged by the statements Jesus made and the question He posed. "You are Israel's teacher, and do you not understand these things?" (John 3:10)

Before we would share the Gospel with others, we need to be captivated by its amazing truths and be prepared to face the radical demands it makes on our own lives.

Pocket Principle

2 **Even though we may have been members of the church for many years, we have to come afresh to the Gospel to examine its claims upon our lives and our relationship with the Lord. We are only motivated to talk about those things which excite us and are significant for us at this point in our lives.**

After reading John 3:16-21, invite group members to describe the various caricatures of the "Gospel" which they at one-time believed themselves, or which they have heard other people express.

In responding to the question, **What would you say to the person who sees the Gospel as Jesus' coming into the world to placate God's anger against sinful humankind?** Bring out the following points:

❑ All three persons of the Trinity are involved in making the Gospel possible.
❑ God the Father conceived the way of salvation.

❑ Jesus Christ came into the world to establish the way back to God through His atoning death and resurrection.

❑ God the Holy Spirit empowered Jesus for His earthly ministry, raised Him from the dead, and works within the sinner's heart.

Pocket Principle

3 The person who shares the Good News must be convinced that the Gospel *is* the power of God for the salvation of *everyone* who believes, no matter how objectionable their personality or difficult their background (Romans 1:16).

As you read and discuss Romans 5:8, 1 Peter 3:18, and 1 John 4:10, bear in mind that group members who have been nurtured in Christian homes and spent their lives in the church may not have seen the radical changes that the Gospel can bring about in the most unlikely of people.

Optional—The Gospel Is Not Just for Nice People

Pre-arrange for a group member who has had a radical conversion experience which completely revolutionized his or her life to share that experience. Or invite a person you know to the group for this opening session to share a testimony.

Reconciled to Others

Sometimes the obstacle to the effective communication of the Gospel lies within the church fellowship or the individual. "Bad news" people cannot convey Good News with credibility. We have first to seek God's help in our straightening out own lives.

GROWING BY DOING   15–20 minutes

Pocket Principle

4 A witness must make it a priority to stay in regular contact with nonchurchgoers and to remain aware of the urgency of their need for the Gospel.

The Same Attitude as Christ
Concern means more than being emotional, it means being prepared to get involved. Urge group members to identify practical ways to involve themselves in the lives of others this week. Share responses to motivate and encourage one another.

Optional—Attitude Adjustment
You may want to pause to express frankly how we feel toward:

☐ unbelievers whose lifestyle we find personally offensive,
☐ the "happy pagan,"
☐ the antagonist who takes every opportunity to ridicule our Christian faith,
☐ the person who is struggling with genuine intellectual obstacles to faith,
☐ nominal Christians, who have a religious upbringing, remain in distant contact with the church, but have no personal relationship with Jesus Christ.

GOING THE SECOND MILE　　　5 minutes

Prayer of Commitment
Encourage group members to complete this section on their own this week. Suggest that they write out their prayer of commitment to seek opportunities to share the Gospel on a 3 x 5 card or piece of paper which they keep as a Bible page marker as a daily reminder.

Points to Remember
Ask group members to be prepared to share at the next meeting three important points from this session which they found to be helpful.

Concerns of Group Members
Encourage a sense of community and mutual support by urging group members to pray for one another this week.

TWO

Expressing Our Gratitude

This lesson is concerned with the issue of motivation. When it comes to evangelism, stress is more often placed on obligation rather than on gratitude. Certainly the Great Commission given by our Lord to His disciples, "Go and make disciples of all nations" (Matthew 28:19), represents a spiritual obligation. But that obligation stems from having received much. Jesus had spent years training His disciples for the task. Having experienced the challenges and privileges of discipleship, they—and we—are then equipped by the Holy Spirit to lead others to share the experience.

SESSION OBJECTIVES

√ To explore ways to ensure that our familiarity with the Gospel does not cause us to take it for granted.

√ To embrace the twin motivations for evangelism: reverential fear of the Lord as the One to whom we are accountable, and the impelling love of Christ to make known the message of reconciliation.

√ To affirm the close biblical tie between worship and witness.

√ To explore the believer's role as an ambassador for Christ.

GETTING ACQUAINTED 20–25 minutes

Have a group member read aloud **A Message Too Important to Keep to Ourselves.** Then use the following activities to create a comfortable, nonthreatening atmosphere.

It's Just What I Wanted!
Help get the conversation going by sharing with the group an incident from your own life when someone showed great generosity to you and how you expressed your gratitude.

"What Do You Say, Junior?"
The comic strip "Family Circus" once showed one child instructing another, "After they give you something, you have to wait till your parents ask, 'What do you say?' Then you say, 'Thank you.' " Invite group members to comment on ways they try to motivate gratitude and its expression.

Taken for Granted
After participants share how they feel when others take them for granted, reflect together on what we are saying to God when we fail to express gratitude for spiritual provisions.

Pocket Principle

1 The believer's response to the Gospel must continually be one of wonder and gratitude.

People who have been brought up in a loving, Christian family and a church fellowship which provided friendship, affirmation, and guidance may take the privilege of their spiritual upbringing for granted. Their attitudes may even extend to the Gospel itself. Emphasize the cost to God of our salvation using the most familiar verse in the Bible, John 3:16.

GAINING INSIGHT 35–40 minutes

Motivation and Methodology
Contrast the resources available to the church today with those available to the early Christians. Those believers were

numerically small, regarded with suspicion, suffered persecution, and had no rapid means of travel or communication technology.

To further emphasize the point, take to the meeting a range of Bible versions, music and teaching cassettes, Yellow Pages listings of churches, advertisements in the weekend edition of the newspaper. Ask the group what they would do if they had none of those things—not even a church building or full-time, trained pastor.

Pocket Principle

2 **The Gospel is most effectively communicated when the entire church membership is mobilized in the constant propagation of its beliefs.**

Before studying 2 Corinthians 5:11–6:2, brainstorm reasons for sharing the Gospel.

When you work through the passage, it will be useful to have people following along with different Bible versions providing different translations of key words. This Bible passage is rich in content, but also contains some difficult verses, so it will be valuable to consult a commentary on the passage before the meeting.

As group members identify key words, allow time to discuss the significance of each, both for Paul's ministry and for our witness today.

Key words and terms include the following:

❑ **fear of the Lord** (5:11)—Paul and his companions knew that they would have to give account to God for their ministry. Were they focusing on vital issues, or being sidetracked into trivia?

❑ **take pride in us** (5:12)—as God's servants who had faithfully brought the message of the Gospel and earnestly sought to live it out consistently.

❑ **Christ's love compels us** (5:14)—The word translated *compels* in the NIV is worth close attention. Ask any group members with other translations to share what those versions say. The KJV has "constraineth us." NRSV has "urges us on," and the REV, "controls us."

- ❑ **convinced that One died for all ... and was raised again** (5:14-15)—Therefore we place our lives under the control of Christ who came to seek and save the lost, and has commissioned us to continue His ministry.
- ❑ **we regard no one from a worldly point of view** (5:16)—rather we see people with the eyes of Christ, realizing what a transformation He could bring about in their lives if they were to be "fresh minted" (PH, paraphrase) by the hand of God.
- ❑ **gave us a ministry of reconciliation** (5:18)—as people who had changed from being enemies to friends of God.
- ❑ **now is the time of God's favor** (6:2)—there will never be a better time, and we must not leave it until the opportunity has passed us by.

Pocket Principle

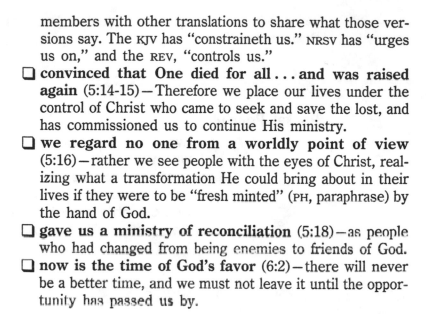

3 Our motivation for evangelism must be biblically grounded, not based on an attempt to satisfy our egos or to ensure the survival of our church by recruiting new members.

At this point invite group members to share personal reasons which inhibit them from sharing their faith. Have they experienced failure or ridicule as they have attempted to witness? Or have they been put off by the way that others have approached them regarding their relationship to Christ?

Worship and Witness
Invite three volunteers to read the verses from the three psalms aloud while the rest of the group follow along. Together discuss the connection between worship and witness, leading group members to recognize that the same gratitude that prompts adoring praise in worship should also prompt us to make known the One whom we praise.

Reconciliation and Relationships
Discuss the questions in this section, then together ask yourselves, "Are we judgmental in our attitudes, or are we pre-

pared to be with the kind of people Paul describes in 1 Corinthians 6:9-11?"

Give specific examples of unlikely people who have become Christians.

Pocket Principle

4 To have confidence in sharing the Gospel, we must really believe that it is "the power of God for the salvation of everyone who believes" (Romans 1:16) no matter how objectionable their present lifestyles, personalities or attitudes.

GROWING BY DOING   15–20 minutes

Praise God
Encourage group members to be specific in their expressions of gratitude, not just for their conversion, but for His present provision.

Tell Others
Set an example of openness by being the first to share.

Examine Relationships
Suggest that group members "see" their "problem" persons as they are at present, and then pray that the Lord will give them a picture of the kind of person He wants to recreate by His grace.

Identify Your Posting
To be effective in sharing the Good News we need the support of fellow Christians. We must pray regularly for one another, and wherever possible, form small groups to demonstrate Christian community and minister in the name of Christ.

GOING THE SECOND MILE   5 minutes

Ministry of Reconciliation

Encourage group members to complete this exercise on their own this week. If they wish, individuals may share with the rest of the group at the next meeting attitudes of which they must repent, because they have created more of an obstacle than a channel for the Gospel.

THREE

Treating a Terminal Condition

In the previous session we considered the motivating force of gratitude to God for all that He has done to secure our salvation. Now we turn our attention to the plight of humanity in its sinful condition, which only the Gospel can remedy.

Pocket Principle

1 Recognize the seriousness of sin both in terms of its all-pervasive influence and of its consequences for the individual and society at large.

SESSION OBJECTIVES

√ To realize the urgency of the evangelistic task.
√ To define *sin* from a comprehensive biblical perspective.
√ To pray: for specific individuals, that group members will have opportunities to share their faith, and that those prayed for will eventually commit their lives to Christ.

GETTING ACQUAINTED   20–25 minutes

Have a group member read aloud **Timely Interventions.**
Then use the following activities to create a comfortable,
nonthreatening atmosphere.

Caring for the Ill
In leading this time of sharing, be sensitive to any group
members who have gone through recent painful experiences
in nursing loved ones.

Sickness and Sin
Sickness has many causes: genetic disorders, tragic acci-
dents, degenerative conditions, and the consequences of poor
diet, lack of exercise, or promiscuous behavior. Salvation
does not bring immunity from sickness, because we continue
to live as part of a fallen world in which the whole of creation
awaits its redemption.

Remember that this is a course on evangelization and not on
the theology of suffering and the healing ministry of the
church. Do not get sidetracked into a prolonged discussion
into the nature and causes of sickness and suffering.

GAINING INSIGHT   35–40 minutes

Two Kinds of Slavery
Ask the group how they would define *sin* as that term is used
in the Bible. The following points need to be drawn out in the
course of conversation:

❑ Sin is missing the mark, falling short of God's standard.
❑ Sin is active or passive rebellion against God's will.
❑ Sin is self-centeredness, rather than service of the other.
❑ Sin is jealousy, hatred, and the demeaning of another
   person.
❑ Sin is refusal to believe in Jesus Christ.

Discuss how the notion of sin is either trivialized or sensa-
tionalized in our culture.

107

Slavery Begins (vv. 17-18)

We witness not only to the offer of forgiveness in the Gospel, but to the power which the Holy Spirit gives by indwelling our lives. We testify to the fact that there has been a radical turn-around in our lives, while at the same time confessing that we still have a long way to go!

Pocket Principle

2 We can take the Good News to others only to the same extent that we have appropriated it for ourselves.

Slavery Develops (v. 19)

Discuss how an impulsive act can become a compulsive habit. Stimulate conversation by discussing the difficulty of finding release from drug or alcohol addiction or chain-smoking. Slavery to sin emphasizes inescapable bondage. The only way out is to accept the release provided by the cross of Christ, to put our complete trust in Him, and obey His every direction in life.

Compare this slavish dependence on Christ to climbing a rock-face under the instruction of an expert climber, who shows us how to tie the rope, use the equipment, and then guides our hands and feet to the secure finger- and toe-holds. After a while we learn to recognize them for ourselves, but we still need to know when to ask for advice and accept correction. To disregard the expert immediately exposes us to danger.

The term **slaves of righteousness** emphasizes the need for consistency, and of Christ's continuing ministry of forgiveness, restoration, and enabling to meet God's requirements. Encourage group discussion on the paradox that only as servants of Christ can we find true freedom. How has this principle been realized in their own walks with God?

Slavery's Result (vv. 20-22)

The final outcome of the two forms of slavery is the logical extension of the lifestyle to which you commit yourself here on earth. Ask the group members how they pictured heaven and hell prior to their own commitment to Christ, or how those two states are understood and joked about among non-Christians.

What are the most common misunderstandings regarding heaven and hell? For example, some represent hell as the place where they will continue to meet with their irreligious friends to continue the fun times they enjoyed on earth—in contrast, heaven must be a boring place!

GROWING BY DOING   15–20 minutes

Deadly Virus
How does the group respond to the concept of sin as a universal and potentially terminal disease? Imagine that you were a team of research doctors: what would be some of your strategies and frustrations in responding to the situation described in the excerpt from McCloskey's book, *Tell It Often— Tell It Well?*

Getting Specific
The formation of prayer groups consisting of three to four persons, meeting to encourage one another in their witness to neighbors and friends, provide accountability, learn through shared experiences, and develop joint evangelistic strategies has proved an effective preparation for many large-scale evangelistic crusades.

Pocket Principle

3 People are not motivated to get involved in evangelism on a long-term basis simply through exhortation. They need training and an ongoing support base.

Provide 3 x 5 inch file cards for each person to write his or her own name and the names of the other people in the prayer group. Then have them list the three names of people who are not yet believers that each member mentions to the prayer group. Covenant to pray for one another and for the not-yet-believers on a daily basis.

GOING THE SECOND MILE 5–10 minutes

Reflection

Suggest that everyone set aside a specific time before the next meeting to reflect upon his or her life, and for the Lord to reveal any obstacles that need to be removed in order to become a more effective witness.

Pocket Principle

4 **A witness not only proclaims the Gospel clearly but lives it convincingly.**

If appropriate, agree to speak frankly with one another of obstacles present in each other's lives. Correction must be given humbly and sensitively and received graciously.

Openness to Opportunity

For subsequent meetings, suggest that everyone keep a written record of the ways in which God has begun to answer the prayers in terms of witnessing opportunities and a growing openness to the Gospel. This will help each member pray more specifically and give thanks in concrete terms.

FOUR

This Is My Story

Newspaper reporters, radio commentators, and TV newscasters are always looking for a human interest angle to the stories they are assigned. People are fascinated by accounts of the experiences of others that stimulate them to relate and identify. That is why personal testimony plays a significant role in the communication of the Good News of Jesus Christ.

The following are among the most common reasons for peoples' reluctance to share their faith.

❑ "I feel awkward in talking about religion with my friends. They wouldn't understand and might think me odd. Religion is such a conversation stopper! My friends might begin to avoid me."

❑ "I know how offended I've been when people try to shove their religion down my throat, and I've seen how other people react when people have tried that in my presence. Their misguided efforts made it all the more difficult to witness to my friends."

❑ "Why should people be interested in my story? Nothing sensational has happened. I live a very ordinary life."

❑ "Even when an opportunity presents itself, I find it difficult to express myself. The words I use among my Christian friends don't seem to mean anything to people who are not involved in church."

Each of these concerns will be addressed during this session and the following one.

SESSION OBJECTIVES

✓ To identify why Christians are reluctant to share their faith stories.

✓ To heighten awareness of the power of personal testimony.

✓ To appreciate that faith-sharing can be undertaken naturally and winsomely.

✓ To begin to articulate our faith with members in the group for mutual encouragement and confidence.

GETTING ACQUAINTED   10–15 minutes

Have a group member read aloud **Sharing My Experience of God's Love,** pausing to list reasons people are reluctant to share their testimonies. Then continue to the following activity.

Word Association
For this exercise you will find it helpful to have available a large sheet of paper and a felt pen to make two lists of words. Draw a vertical line down the center of the paper and at the head of the left-hand column write *EVANGELIST.*

You will probably discover that the word *evangelist* has negative connotations for most people. If the group focuses on a biblical understanding or relates it to their own personal appreciation for the work of particular evangelists, sharpen the approach by asking them how their unchurched friends would respond.

Having completed the first part of the word association exercise, write at the head of the right-hand column *CHRISTIAN FRIEND,* then go around the circle inviting each member to share with the group the person who has been most influential in helping him or her to know God personally. Ask each person what adjective would describe that person. Note the contrast in the two lists.

Pocket Principle

1 **People are most likely to be helped spiritually by those who come alongside as a friend, rather than through teachers with a lecturing approach, or those who come across as salespersons!**

GAINING INSIGHT   35–40 minutes

In this session we are going to consider two testimonies recorded in the Bible, one from the New Testament and the other from the Old. We are taking two, rather than confining ourselves to one story, in order to appreciate that there is no one standard approach for sharing our testimonies. Divide the group. Group One will study the conversion of the Apostle Paul. Group Two will study Psalm 23. If your group is too small or reluctant to divide, you can remain together to study both sections. In order to save time, take the Acts passage as a whole, rather than in the phases given. You will also need to omit some of the questions.

Paul's Conversion
PHASE ONE: Paul's Preconversion Life
Paul has the credentials to establish his credibility. Although born in the province of Cilicia, he was brought up in Jerusalem where he received the best of religious training under the renowned teacher Gamaliel. He had been a zealous persecutor of the fledgling church, a fact well known among the highest Jewish officials.

PHASE TWO: Paul's Conversion
As you discuss the chart, emphasize that in order to have a genuine conversion we don't need to be confronted by a blinding light, be thrown to the ground, and hear a voice from heaven.

113

Pocket Principle

2 Recognize the fact that people come to Christ in a multitude of ways. While some individuals can point to a single dramatic turning point, for many people conversion has been a more gradual process.

But we do need life-changing encounters, an ongoing relationship with God, and to recognize our need to receive ministry from our Christian brothers and sisters. We must also recognize that conversion leads to a call to minister to others in Christ's name.

PHASE THREE: Paul's Postconversion
In discussing the problems which new believers might encounter that prevent them feeling welcomed by the church, encourage honesty. Many mature believers who have been brought up in the church are unaware of the existence of the problem.

The following questions will help to sharpen the discussion:

❏ How many conversions to Christ have occurred through our church during the past year?
❏ How many first-time visitors do we get each month, and what percentage return?
❏ What steps do we take to help the new believer build on that initial commitment, and how effective is that process?

The Shepherd's Psalm
This is probably the most well-known passage in the Old Testament. For this reason it can help people recognize the importance of bearing witness to the ways in which God has related to them in the various experiences of life. The psalmist speaks of times of weariness, fear, and danger. The fact that God's presence guided, refreshed, protected, and provided establishes a basis of hope for the future.

Pocket Principle

3 Testimony giving must not become stereotypical. Each person has a different story to tell of the manifold grace of God.

114

> Our story can encourage the hard-pressed believers as well as challenge the unbeliever.

When the two groups have concluded their studies, bring them together to share the three most important points they discovered.

In order to emphasize the fact that our witness is as much concerned with our present relationship with God as with a dramatic turning-point in the distant past, you may want to pause briefly to share what God has meant to you this past week.

GROWING BY DOING   35–40 minutes

Sharing Our Stories

After the testimony-sharing time in pairs, bring two pairs together to make groups of four people. Tell each person to take no more than three minutes to share with the others the testimony that they heard, not their own.

Pocket Principle

4 **People talk about those issues that excite them and that they have the confidence to share. Therefore, encourage people, on a regular basis, to share what God is doing in their lives. As they become accustomed to doing this in the fellowship of believers, they are more likely to build confidence to share their witness with the people they encounter who are not yet believers.**

Emphasize the point that listening to someone else tell your story helps you to realize what was most significant and which points you did not express clearly.

Prayer Groups

Be sure that each person has a list of the persons for whom they will all be praying. Covenant to pray for one another and for the Lord's enabling to share His love and explain the Good News.

GOING THE SECOND MILE   5–10 minutes

Write Your Testimony
Encourage members to write out and practice their testimonies this week.

Pray for Opportunities
Remind members to continue to pray for openings to share their faith.

Pray for People
In preparation for the prayer groups, make copies of the following chart for each person so that they have a written record of the persons for whom they have promised to pray.

MY PRAYER PARTNERS	PERSONS FOR WHOM WE ARE PRAYING
Self	1. _____
	2. _____
	3. _____
	4. _____
_____	5. _____
	6. _____
	7. _____
_____	8. _____
	9. _____

Permission to photocopy for use in group study granted.

FIVE

Whom Do I Know?

Many churches are so preoccupied with trying to reach the wider community that they overlook the extensive social network with whom the congregation is already in contact. This session focuses on the opportunity and challenge of reaching those whom we already know.

The basic premise of this session is that the people with whom we are in regular contact represent our primary mission field. As we show a concern for the spiritual and personal well-being of those people, and seek to be a consistent, effective witness to Christ among them, God will open up wider opportunities for witness. The movement of mission is from the local to the global (Acts 1:8).

SESSION OBJECTIVES

✓ To affirm our ability to witness to our personal experience of Jesus despite our limitations.

✓ To see people around us with the "eyes of faith" as the transformed people they could become were they to commit their lives to Christ.

✓ To commit to witnessing to the people we already know and care about.

GETTING ACQUAINTED   15–20 minutes

Have a group member read aloud **Starting Close to Home.**
Then use the following activity to help create a comfortable
atmosphere.

May I Introduce . . .
Try to prevent this exercise from becoming "religious" by
relating an everyday incident outside of the church context. The more light-hearted this opening sharing time, the
better!

Likening the task of the evangelism to that of making introductions can help to remove many misconceptions. It
counters the notion that we must be pushy by emphasizing
the need for politeness. It reminds us to slip into the background rather than interposing ourselves between the person
and Christ. We are not expected to know the answer to every
question or objection. We are simply those who know God
personally in Jesus Christ, and are concerned that others
should know God on the same terms.

When everyone has shared, distinguish between those introductions that had no discernable, long-term consequences
and those that had significant impact. Also reflect on the
possibility of an introduction made many months, or even
years, previously subsequently bearing unexpected fruit.

GAINING INSIGHT   35–40 minutes

John Introduces Jesus
The primary task of the evangelist is to point people to Jesus,
not to pressure them to join our church or our fellowship
group.

Pocket Principle

1 The task of the evangelist is not to attempt to "play God," but simply to be a
witness.

The Scripture passages chosen for this session demonstrate that we do not have to know all the answers or to have worked out a systematic theology to be effective in our witness. The essential qualifications to fulfill our role is an authentic relationship with Jesus Christ as Savior and Lord. We witness as those who are continuing in the school of discipleship, not as those who have graduated from the class!

The Samaritan woman made such an impact on her community, not because of what she knew, but because of the experience which she recounted, the invitation she gave, and the question she raised (John 4:29-30). She did all the right things without having attended a single class on "How to Share Your Testimony"!

In your discussion of the demon-possessed man, notice that the man reached a far wider audience than his family and friends. He told his story throughout the *Decapolis,* which translated, means *the Ten Cities.*

Pocket Principle

2 New converts often make the most effective witnesses, especially during the first six months of their Christian life.

Andrew Finds Cephas

The question Jesus asked John and Andrew as He turned to see them following Him is significant. In asking them, "What do you want?" He was inviting them to state their purpose, and their response was both straightforward and significant.

The disciples simply asked, "Where are You staying?" They had a lot of questions to ask. They wanted to know how they could keep in contact with Jesus. Realizing what lay behind their questions, Jesus gave an entirely appropriate response, "Come and see." What was the implication behind His invitation?

People likewise respond to our witness to Christ in various ways, showing degrees of readiness for a wide variety of reasons. We must constantly ask ourselves, "What are their needs right now? What do they need to know?" We must be careful not to overload people with more information than they are able to receive, or to pressure them to make a commitment prematurely.

The checklist in this section will probably indicate that people initially come to Christ trying to find answers to a whole range of needs. When we first hear the Gospel, it is often in relation to our specific circumstances. For that reason, we need to hear the Gospel stated a number of times in a variety of ways. Then our understanding will expand and the Gospel will continue to challenge us as we hear the testimony of others to God's grace in their lives.

Pocket Principle

3 We should present the Gospel in ways that are relevant to people's varied needs, without the message being conditioned by those needs. Ultimately, the Gospel is concerned with the questions that God addresses to us, rather than the questions that we bring to God.

Discuss the significance of the giving of new names: from Saul to Paul, and from Simon to Cephas. A new name signifies a transformed character brought about by the Holy Spirit working in a person's life. A powerful motivation for witness is to try to see the people around us not as they are, but as they might become through the power of the Gospel.

Philip Finds Nathanael
Jesus told Nathanael that before he was aware of Jesus, Jesus was aware of him. It is always God who initiates the search, although we are often not aware of it at the time. Whatever the circumstances, and however unexpected the opportunity, we must remind ourselves that God got there before we did!

GROWING BY DOING   25–30 minutes

Reflection
Encourage honesty in the group discussions. Relieve people of the need to feel that they have to manufacture a "success

story." There is as much to be learned from our failures and frustrations as from our successes.

Role Play

The role-play exercise provides the first attempt to get beyond a generic testimony to one that relates to the life situation of a particular individual. Instruct the group members to ask any clarifying questions they have in order to picture the individual more clearly. They must make every effort to be that person, and to ask if what is being said is both understandable and relevant. Invite them to explain unfamiliar "religious" words and terms.

Address the specific questions listed in this section. Emphasize that this is a learning exercise for everyone in the group. We don't expect stellar performances from each other. After receiving the comments, we can think how we might communicate more effectively with that individual when God provides the opportunity or nudges us into taking the initiative.

GOING THE SECOND MILE   5–10 minutes

Rewrite Your Testimony

The discipline of writing out a testimony after the role-play exercise helps reinforce the valuable points, and to incorporate them in a revised version while, at the same time, ensuring that each person is still telling his or her story in a way that is natural for him or her. Encourage the group members to review the points made at the end of the lesson as a guide in this exercise.

Get Feedback

Urge group members to "field test" their testimonies in this way.

Keep Praying

Some group members find it helpful to keep a private diary of their prayer group's experiences of witnessing and seeing the evidence of God at work in the lives of the persons for whom they have covenanted to pray.

SIX

Taking Time

Overcautious types are likely to be hindered from making any significant move until every question has been answered to their complete satisfaction. The impetuous person will not stop to consider the implications of a decision until he or she is brought up short by harsh reality.

Impetuosity must not be confused with faith. One of the obvious distinctions is that the former wilts as it encounters obstacles, while the latter grows as those obstacles are confronted. Authentic faith is committed for the long haul.

SESSION OBJECTIVES

√ To recognize that people come to Christ in different ways; some come quickly, others more slowly.
√ To define what it means to be born again.
√ To meditate on the role of the fruit of the Spirit in our witnessing.

GETTING ACQUAINTED   15–20 minutes

Have a group member read aloud **Balancing Urgency with Patience.** Then use the following activity to help create a comfortable atmosphere for this session.

Meeting Mr./Ms. Right
The objective in our evangelistic efforts is not to pressure people into making a decision but to lead them into a relationship. This exercise is designed to make us aware that indepth human relationships begin in different ways and develop at varying speeds.

Many successful marriages that have stood the test of time did not begin with "love at first sight"! Likewise, we must not be put off if people we woo for Christ at first appear to show little interest. As in any relationship-building situation, it is usually counter-productive to try to force the pace.

GAINING INSIGHT   35–40 minutes

No Hard Sell
Jesus' encounter with Nicodemus, recorded in John 3, is a classic text on evangelism. There is a danger that our over-familiarity with the story will blind us to the significance of some of the most important details. Introduce the study as an "action replay" with your hand on the pause button!

The most frequent misuse of the passage is to emphasize Jesus' statement **You must be born again** (v. 7), in such a way that an immediate decision is called for. This runs contrary to the passage. Furthermore, it should be noted that the **you** is plural and not singular. Jesus is emphasizing the necessity for Israel as a whole to be "reborn."

Some people who have been avoiding important spiritual issues for years need time to think through the implication of what you have said. Those people with little background knowledge or who are filled with misconceptions regarding the nature of God and the Gospel may need a number of sessions to work through issues and gain a more adequate understanding of biblical teaching in these areas before they can make a firmly-based decision.

Pocket Principle

1 Tell people only as much as they are able to take in, and give them time to process what they have heard.

With some inquirers the best approach is to invite their questions and ask them questions rather than simply making statements. However, in this instance, Jesus cuts across Nicodemus' opening remarks with a blunt statement.

List the range of opinions concerning the person of Christ mentioned by the group, and then discuss how to introduce the Gospel in response to those views. What would be your opening lines? Don't spend time developing comprehensive responses—this will come later in the course!

Born-Again Christians

Although the term "born-again" is familiar in North American society, its biblical meaning and significance is unclear to many people. Explain that *born again* can equally be translated *born from above.* Why do you think Jesus used that imagery on this occasion? To be born signifies a fresh start in life. To be born from above indicates that God must be in at the beginning to bring us into His kingdom. We can never make it on our own by endeavoring to fulfill the requirement of the Law, a mistaken notion common among the Pharisees.

Other useful references: John 1:11-13; Titus 3:4-7; James 1:17-18; 1 Peter 1:3-5, 23.

The phrase **"born of water and of the Spirit"** is variously interpreted. Some take "water" to refer to semen or to birth waters, but to say that physical birth is necessary for new birth is simply to state the obvious. A more likely interpretation is that "water" here refers to baptism, signifying cleansing from sin following repentance. For Nicodemus, "born of water" would signify the kind of baptism performed by John or by the disciples of Jesus.

125

"Born of the Spirit" has a future reference, pointing to the regenerating and empowering presence of the Spirit made accessible through the sending of the Spirit following our Lord's ascension into heaven.

Considering the religious obstacles and social barriers that Nicodemus the Pharisee and member of the ruling council had to face, it is no wonder that Nicodemus asked, "How can a man be born when he is old?" In other words, how can he start all over again? Try to put yourselves into Nicodemus' place. Then look at verses 7 and 8, and discuss their significance for Nicodemus.

Pocket Principle

2 Take care when using well-known religious terminology to ensure that you and the person with whom you are communicating have an accurate understanding of the term. Be aware that some terms may be an obstacle to communication because they have acquired negative connotations.

Invite group members to consider the people for whom they are praying to come to Christ. What are the inhibiting factors in their lives? Does our awareness of those obstacles cause us to think it is of little use trying to share the Gospel with them? If so, what do verses 7 and 8 have to say to us?

The exercise relating to the supernatural and unpredictable nature of our encounter with God works best when one or more persons in the group were previously unchurched or had badly messed up their lives. If your group consists of people who have been nurtured all their lives within the Christian community, widen the discussion to include people they know whom they considered to be unlikely converts.

Look and Live
Jesus compares the fatal consequences of being bitten by a snake to the equally serious consequences of rejecting

Christ. Spiritual death is total exclusion from the kingdom and very presence of God.

The lifting up of the Son of man refers to the crucifixion of Christ (see John 12:31-32). His death for the sins of the world offers the only hope of salvation from the consequences of sin.

Pocket Principle

3 **Any statement of the Gospel must focus on the identity of Jesus Christ and the uniqueness and vital nature of the work He accomplished for the salvation of humankind.**

 GROWING BY DOING   30–35 minutes

Fruitful Believers

"In and through Jesus the future kingdom has become a present reality; He, as it were, is the kingdom in microcosm, and thus vital contact with Him is contact with the kingdom of God. And vital contact with the kingdom means that we as trusting servants come under the gracious, saving, and fatherly rule of God" (Peter Toon, *Born Again, A Biblical and Theological Study of Regeneration,* Baker, 1987, p. 27).

As you emphasize the necessity of being born again, explain that this does not mean you must have a dramatic, crisis experience, or be able to name a time and place. You simply have to know that you are alive!

Many people who claim to be born again exhibit little evidence of spiritual growth. The believer is meant to grow in stature "and become mature, attaining to the whole measure of the fullness of Christ" (Ephesians 4:13).

The one-sentence prayers are intended to make us aware that our lives need to be consistent with our message. We must demonstrate some of the benefits the message has brought in our lives.

127

Prayer Groups
The purpose of the prayer groups is to encourage one another to be patient, believing that in God's time we will see the people for whom we are praying eventually respond to the call of Christ.

GOING THE SECOND MILE 5–10 minutes

Scripture Memory
Urge everyone to commit John 1:12-13 to memory.

Outreach Events
Encourage the group to think of a series of steps it might take to develop long-term strategies to reach people, especially those who seem unresponsive at present.

SEVEN

Cross Talk

Attempting to explain the Gospel to persons who have never heard it before and have no knowledge of the Bible presents one set of challenges, while sharing the Good News with those who have heard it before and have had prior exposure to the Bible and the church presents a different set of challenges.

In the former case, it is not so much fresh information people need as a fresh approach to motivate them to reexamine what they think they already know. Even more to the point, they might require, above all else, to be enveloped by people who are seeking to live out their beliefs in a loving and natural way, rather than be challenged and exhorted.

In the latter case, we must assume nothing and explain every biblical term and concept carefully. We also have to find points of contact with the other person's worldview so that the message makes sense.

Pocket Principle

1 **We should not be so preoccupied with what we want to say that we fail to give careful consideration to what the person needs to hear about the nature of God and the Gospel.**

Sometimes the Holy Spirit moves people by confronting them with the truth of the Gospel, which then leads them to experience the abundant life in Christ. Other people are first surrounded by a loving Christian community, or meet a caring disciple of Christ, and then develop a spiritual appetite to know the truth. Be prepared for the Holy Spirit to work either way!

SESSION OBJECTIVES

√ To recognize that the Gospel can be presented in a variety of ways, according to the understanding and needs of the individual.

√ To focus our presentation of the Gospel on the person of Jesus Christ: His life, His atoning death, and His resurrection and ascension.

√ To examine the role of each of the three Persons of the Trinity in providing for our salvation.

√ To learn three simple ways to explain the Gospel, each appropriate to a particular kind of person.

GETTING ACQUAINTED 20–25 minutes

Have a group member read aloud **Ways to Present the Gospel.** Then use the following activity to help create a comfortable atmosphere for this session.

Sales Talk

A salesperson with integrity and skill will assess the customer before attempting to make the sale. Some customers are knowledgable. They come to the store knowing a great deal about the performance capabilities, quality, and reliability of the full range of models and of the reputations of the various manufacturers. Others are discerning customers, who may not have much technical knowledge, but have carefully assessed their needs, and will not buy unless the model meets their requirements.

Other customers want an item, but have not done their research or considered their needs in any detail. The unscrupulous salesperson can sell them more than they need or dump inferior items which he wants to clear from stock.

Unscrupulous tactics of salespersons might include:

❑ pushiness, giving customers no time to browse;
❑ such eagerness to go through their sales pitch that they do not take time to listen;
❑ a display of expertise designed to impress customers who have no idea or interest in the technical specifications and no understanding of the terminology used;
❑ a desperate attempt to close the deal and make a sale to meet their monthly sales goals rather than working in the best interests of customers.

Paul says that we must not be "peddlers of God's Word" (2 Corinthians 2:17). We are not unscrupulous salespersons trying to corner people into making premature and badly informed decisions, or to palm off inferior products.

Pocket Principle

2 The way to approach another person is the way in which we would want another person to approach us.

GAINING INSIGHT   25–40 minutes

Near and Far

In his insightful book on conversion entitled *Turning to God* (Baker, 1989), David Wells draws a helpful distinction between "insider" and "outsider" conversions. Or, to use the Apostle Paul's language, between those who are *near* and those who are *far off*.

In New Testament times, the outsiders—those who were far off—were the Gentiles who needed to hear the Gospel, whereas the Jewish followers of Jesus were the "insiders" in terms of God's covenant promises.

This remains a helpful distinction in our day. Some of our

evangelism will be directed toward "insiders"—those persons who have had previous contact with the church and have some knowledge of the Bible and exposure to the Gospel. The challenge is to commit themselves to what they already know; to translate knowledge into belief and belief into behavior.

Pocket Principle

3 In seeking to explain the Gospel, it is important to try to identify the particular obstacles which hinder understanding and readiness to surrender to Christ.

Divide the group into two subgroups so that each can study a Scripture passage: one passage will describe how the Gospel was communicated to Jews, and the other to Gentiles.

If the group is too small to subdivide, or wishes to remain as one group, you can either select one or other of the Bible studies, or consider them both sequentially.

"Insider" Conversion
In Galatians 2:15-21 Paul addresses the problem of the Gospel becoming undermined by legalism, a common danger in Christian communities made up predominantly of Jewish believers.

To further elucidate the question, you might want to ask, "On what grounds do people consider themselves as Christians in our society?"

"Outsider" Conversion
To be *dead* means to be separated from God's presence and to be deaf to His Word or unresponsive to His will. Draw attention to the hopelessness of the human condition apart from Christ.

Satan operates:

☐ around us—so that we follow the ways of this world;
☐ above us—so that we succumb to the rule of the kingdom of the air;

132

❏ within us—so that we yield to the spirit who is now at work in those who are disobedient.

People who came into the fellowship of believers out of a pagan society, like those at Ephesus or Corinth, did not come "ready laundered." It was only by the grace of God that their lives could be cleaned up (see 1 Corinthians 6:9-11). We must resist the temptation to idealize the church in New Testament times. Paul's letters deal with a wide range of serious moral problems, as well as theological confusion and pastoral issues.

Have we rubbed shoulders with people with whom we have felt uncomfortable, and made it clear, either by hints or in a forthright manner, that they were unwelcome?

Pocket Principle

4 We must refrain from confronting every person we are seeking to win to Christ with *our* moral agenda, and be sensitive to the issues which the Holy Spirit is addressing in a person's life. God may be wanting to deal with one issue at a time according to His own priority-listing and timetable.

GROWING BY DOING   30–35 minutes

Cross Talk Guidelines

Those who want to share the Gospel frequently encounter two problems. The first is that they have learned only one way to do it, so that they feel "programmed" and unnatural. The second is that many Gospel presentations are so complicated, requiring the person to learn a succession of steps and accompanying verses, that they never get started for fear of not being able to finish!

The two sample presentations are each geared to a particular kind of person, and each is based on just one Bible passage. If we are to make a start in our witness it is best to keep it as simple as possible. We can always elaborate later as our experience and confidence grow.

It may be helpful for group members to work in pairs on each presentation and then to share their combined effort with the other group members. Working with someone else may prove helpful to those who find it particularly difficult to put themselves in the shoes of a nonbeliever, and sharing with the group will lead to mutual enrichment as ideas are pooled. As with the witnessing exercise of the previous session, to make an initial presentation in a safe environment can build confidence to later share with the intended recipient.

Presentation to a "Churched" Person

It is important to spend time unpacking the biblical vocabulary so that we can explain unfamiliar concepts or those where there is widespread misunderstanding.

Presentation to a Secularized Person

After completing this section, take time to discuss outreach ideas that group members came up with in response to last session's **Going the Second Mile.** The next session will challenge the group to put some of these ideas into action.

Pocket Principle

5 In training to share the Gospel, keep a particular individual in mind, and ask yourself, "Would I ever say this kind of thing to that individual?" Work at it until you feel both comfortable with the thought of sharing it, and convinced that it is what the person needs to hear.

GOING THE SECOND MILE 5–10 minutes

Witnessing Tool

You may want to obtain some copies of the "Steps to Peace with God" booklet beforehand and make them available to the group members to share among their friends, as they have opportunity, during the remainder of the course.

Scripture Helps

Ask group members if they have a specific person in mind who is lonely, fearful, or guilt-ridden. If so, invite them to work on an additional way of presenting the Gospel along the same lines as they have followed in this session.

EIGHT

It Takes a Community to Communicate

I have a hunch that the effectiveness of any training course is in direct proportion to its brevity and practical application! In other words, the longer the course, and the more complex we make the issues, the more people are intimidated. They lose nerve rather than gain boldness as the trainer describes every possible kind of scenario and every difficulty which could possibly arise.

With this in mind, some trainers operate according to the principle that it is preferable to train after the event rather than in anticipation of an occasion which never materializes.

The best motivation for doing evangelism is to see and, if possible, be part of an effective outreach program. After all, Jesus trained His own disciples on the observation/participation/ reflection/delegation model.

Pocket Principle

1 The two basic principles in training are:
  1. There is little point in saying it until people need to know it.
  2. Learn a little and practice a lot, rather than learn a lot and then never put it into practice.

SESSION OBJECTIVES

√ To translate theory into practice by encouraging individual initiative in sharing the Gospel and holding one another accountable.

√ To plan and implement a joint outreach venture among a selected group of friends and acquaintances whom we believe to be ready to be brought into a fellowship of Christians and challenged by the Gospel.

√ To seek the renewing and enabling power of the Holy Spirit to direct our witness and help us be authentic and effective.

√ To examine our group activities and our church program to assess how we can increase our effectiveness in welcoming inquirers and helping new believers become established in their faith and grow in Christ.

GETTING ACQUAINTED   15–20 minutes

Have a group member read aloud **The Impact of Corporate Witness.** Then use the following activity to launch this session.

Under the Influence

Persuasion is an everyday experience as we share our various enthusiasms and concerns. This opening exercise focuses on the range of motivational factors which cause us to respond to a persuasive person or group. Once again, try to steer the group away from religious and church-related examples.

GAINING INSIGHT   35–40 minutes

Community in Small Groups

In studying the Acts 2 passage, try not to become focused on the supernatural phenomena. This was a unique circumstance, and this aspect is entirely in God's hands anyway— He will do what He will do!

The key factors for our study are:

❑ The group was spending time with God, coming to know Jesus in a new way as the ascended Lord who had breathed His Holy Spirit upon them.

❑ Their experience of the Holy Spirit was so powerful that they left the security and seclusion of their room to declare the works of God in the most strategic location in Jerusalem.

❑ They spoke in the languages represented by the international gathering of pilgrims from around the Mediterranean world. The Good News was not confined to the Jewish pilgrims but was also for the people to whom they would return.

Pocket Principle

1 The Holy Spirit is poured out on all believers, irrespective of age, sex, and social standing, in order that the Word of God might be proclaimed everywhere.

Outreach through Small Groups
Consider the need for a small-group network to be in place, ready to receive a large number of inquirers and new believers.

How would you describe your church:

❑ **fortress** that keeps out "the enemy" and undesirables?
❑ **private club** that screens potential members?
❑ **theater** that attracts a critical and fickle clientele?
❑ **lighthouse** that is visible enough to attract all in distress?
❑ **network** that provides multiple access points, where people can encounter the fellowship of believers?

Which model most closely fits the one describes in Acts 2:42-47?

One of the most significant developments in mainline churches during the past twenty-five years has been the mul-

138

tiplication of home-based Bible study, prayer, and fellowship groups. However, very few of these groups have included intentional evangelism as part of their vision. How do you explain this omission?

In response to your study of the two Bible passages, and assuming that your group intends to continue after the course, or that the members will continue in other fellowship groups, what should be the balance of activities?

GROWING BY DOING   20–25 minutes

Look Ahead

Discuss with your pastor or church board your plans to invite your friends, neighbors, and colleagues to a Sunday worship service. In what ways might that service be specifically geared to be a welcoming and informative guest service?

Look Back

Allow time for sharing and closure.

GOING THE SECOND MILE   5–10 minutes

Plan an Outreach Meeting

If the group is sufficiently motivated, determine to implement a plan, with dates agreed and responsibilities allocated to various group members. Arrange a follow-up planning meeting to go over the details. Hold the event, or series of meetings, and then meet again to evaluate your efforts. What worked? What didn't work? What would you do differently next time?

If you succeed in attracting a group of new people so that you have now become too large, arrange for two or three of the original group members to go with the new people and start a new group. Don't talk in terms of splitting the group, but of *birthing* a new one!